Teaching Primary Programming with Scratch

Pupil Book – Year 4

PHIL BAGGE

A research informed scheme of work by Phil Bagge HIAS Computing Inspector/Advisor
Part of the HIAS Teaching Primary Programming from Scratch Series

Published in 2023 by University of Buckingham Press,
an imprint of Legend Times Group
51 Gower Street
London WC1E 6HJ
info@unibuckinghampress.com
www.unibuckinghampress.com

Published by arrangement with Hampshire Inspection and Advisory Service (part of Hampshire County Council)

ISBN 978-1-91505-4-241

CONTENTS

If you are struggling for time, I would recommend you do **Toy Give Away** or **Regular 2D shapes** and either **Fish Tank** or **Helicopter Game**.

INTRODUCTION & PROGRESSION

INTRODUCTION

What Does This Book Do?

This book is a complete scheme of work for teaching primary programming using Scratch in Year 4 for 8–9 year olds.

What Is Included?

It includes permission to photocopy the pupil worksheets for your class or school.

These are clearly marked on the top right of the page.

It includes links to example code, project templates and slides to improve how you teach primary programming.

Part of a Series

It is part of a five-book series. Three other books include projects for other year groups.

Teaching Primary Programming with Scratch, Year 3

Teaching Primary Programming with Scratch, Year 5

Teaching Primary Programming with Scratch, Year 6

Teaching Primary programming with Scratch – Research-Informed Approaches

The teacher book explores methodology and pedagogy in detail helping you to understand why an approach is useful.

Progression

There is a clear, research-informed progression through the series and the grey-backed code shows which programming concepts are introduced in this book.

My Pupils have not used Scratch before

If pupils have a knowledge of the Scratch programming environment then they can start here. If they don't have this essential information I recommend you start with a couple of projects from Book 1 first. Pupils cannot use PRIMM methodology correctly until they understand simple sequence and the programming environment.

Pedagogy in a Few Paragraphs

Introduction to Programming Concepts Away From Code

Pupils are taught key programming concepts away from programming to lower cognitive load and make it easier to transfer these ideas from one programming language to another. They can record their algorithms on the knowledge organiser.

Paired Programming

Pupils are encouraged to work in same ability pairs for some parts of the projects because this has shown to be particularly helpful for pupils working within or below the expected outcomes.

PRIMM

Pupils are encouraged to read and understand code before they create their own code. We use the PRIMM method in this book.

Predict

Run

Investigate

Modify (change)

Make

Parsons

Four out of the five modules include a Parsons exercise to build code from a plan and pre-selected code. This can be useful for SEN pupils.

Creative

Each project provides time and stimulus to be creative in code within the zone of proximal development provided by the taught concepts and explored projects. In other words, it has reasonable projects that can be created independently or with minimum teacher support.

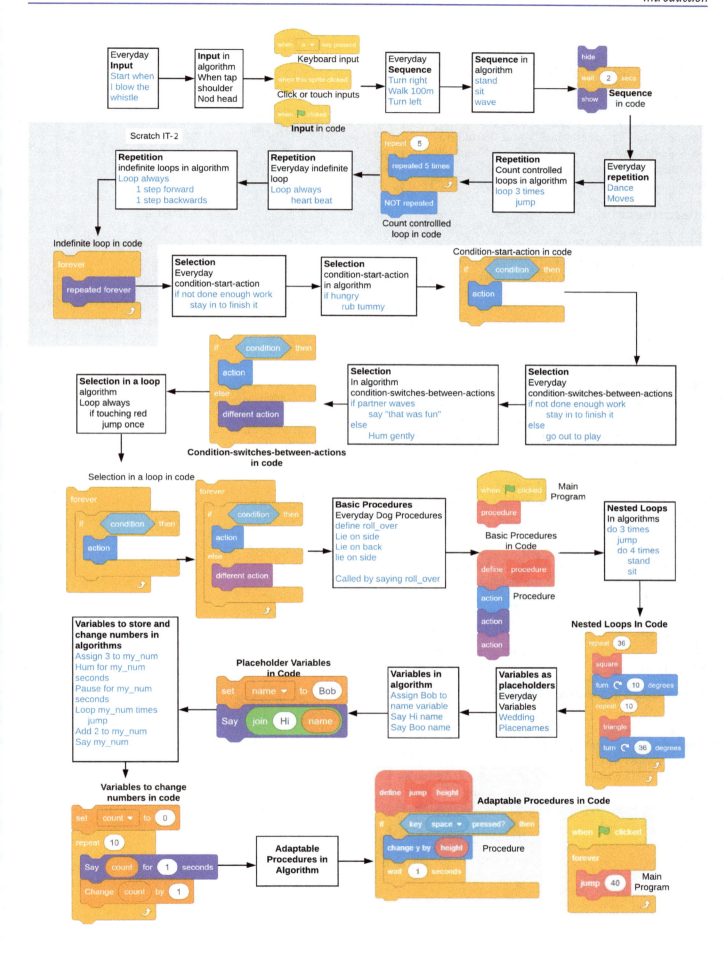

Everyday **Input**
Start when
I blow the whistle

Input in algorithm
When tap shoulder
Nod head

when a key pressed
Keyboard input

when this sprite clicked
Click or touch inputs

when clicked
Input in code

Everyday **Sequence**
Turn right
Walk 100m
Turn left

Sequence in algorithm
stand
sit
wave

hide
wait 2 secs
show
Sequence in code

Scratch IT-2

Repetition
indefinite loops in algorithm
Loop always
1 step forward
1 step backwards

Repetition
Everyday indefinite loop
Loop always
heart beat

repeat 5
repeated 5 times
NOT repeated
Count controlled loop in code

Repetition
Count controlled loops in algorithm
loop 3 times
jump

Everyday **repetition**
Dance Moves

Indefinite loop in code

forever
repeated forever

Selection
Everyday
condition-start-action
if not done enough work
stay in to finish it

Selection
condition-start-action in algorithm
if hungry
rub tummy

Condition-start-action in code
if condition then
action

Selection in a loop
algorithm
Loop always
if touching red
jump once

if condition then
action
else
different action

Selection
In algorithm
condition-switches-between-actions
if partner waves
say "that was fun"
else
Hum gently

Condition-switches-between-actions in code

Selection
Everyday
condition-switches-between-actions
if not done enough work
stay in to finish it
else
go out to play

Selection in a loop in code

forever
if condition then
action

forever
if condition then
action
else
different action

Basic Procedures
Everyday Dog Procedures
define roll_over
Lie on side
Lie on back
lie on side

Called by saying roll_over

when clicked
procedure
Main Program

Basic Procedures in Code
define procedure
action
action
action
Procedure

Nested Loops
In algorithms
do 3 times
jump
do 4 times
stand
sit

Nested Loops In Code
repeat 36
square
turn 10 degrees
repeat 10
triangle
turn 36 degrees

Variables to store and change numbers in algorithms
Assign 3 to my_num
Hum for my_num seconds
Pause for my_num seconds
Loop my_num times
jump
Add 2 to my_num
Say my_num

Placeholder Variables in Code
set name to Bob
Say join Hi name

Variables in algorithm
Assign Bob to name variable
Say Hi name
Say Boo name

Variables as placeholders
Everyday Variables
Wedding Placenames

Variables to change numbers in code
set count to 0
repeat 10
Say count for 1 seconds
Change count by 1

Adaptable Procedures in Algorithm

define jump height
if key space pressed? then
change y by height
wait 1 seconds
Procedure

Adaptable Procedures in Code

when clicked
forever
jump 40
Main Program

7

Knowledge

Key knowledge is introduced in the concept introductions and reinforced in each of the activities.

Revisiting Learning

It is important to revisit prior learning, so each module has questions and activities which revise learning from Year 3 on sequence and as we move from count-controlled loops to indefinite loops, prior loops are used and referenced to revisit learning.

Assessment

Summative Assessment

Summative assessment is baked into every stage of the PRIMM process, providing a wealth of data to determine progress.

Self–Assessment

Pupils self-mark to help them see how they have progressed, reducing teacher workload and enabling teachers to concentrate on pupils that need more support.

Hints & Tips

Every pupil's resource also includes a copy of the resource annotated with extra information to further teachers' programming knowledge, hints and formative assessment opportunities in case pupils are stuck and tips to adapt or support whole class teaching.

Many of these extra hints and tips will not be needed, but the more informed the teacher is, the better quality learning opportunity pupils will have.

Can We Start Here?

Pupils could start here if they have prior Scratch environmental knowledge. Agency over sprite, background and sound creation. The ability to snap blocks and delete code. If your pupils have not used Scratch before, I recommend starting with

Teaching Primary Programming with Scratch, Year 3

which uses different pedagogy appropriate to pupils prior knowledge.

Committed to Improvements

HIAS, Hampshire's Inspection & Advisory Service, is committed to developing and improving these resources. We recognize that primary programming is still its infancy in comparison with other subjects and that new research and primary practice will refine and improve teaching and learning in this area. All royalties earned from this series will be used to write more computing books and revise these resources as needed.

Photocopiable resource for pupils

Teacher Hints & Tips on the same photocopiable resource

WE ARE LEARNING ABOUT
LOOPS IN ALGORITHMS AND PROGRAMMING

Count-controlled loop algorithm

A loop is any set of instructions that are repeated

A count-controlled loop

Can replace a sequence where there is a pattern.

Is controlled by the number

Ends after the number of repeats are complete

Is called a repeat loop in Scratch programming

Has a flow of control

A flashing light is often programmed using an indefinite loop as shown below

Algorithms

A set of instructions or rules to do something

Algorithms can be used to plan non-programming events such as exercise

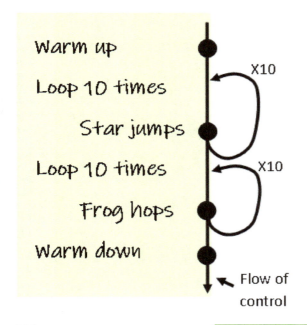

Warm up

Loop 10 times   X10

   Star jumps

Loop 10 times   X10

   Frog hops

Warm down

← Flow of control

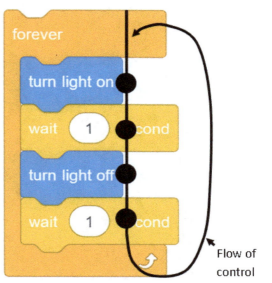

Flow of control

Indefinite loop algorithm

We are

Indenting to show what instructions are inside a loop when writing planning algorithms.

Loop Vocabulary

repeat, loop, iterate, do so many times

An infinite indefinite loop

Can replace a sequence where there is a pattern.

Only ends when the digital device is turned off

Is called a forever loop in Scratch programming

Has a flow of control or order; the instructions are carried out

Is called an indefinite loop because we do not know how many times it will repeat

photocopiable page

INTRODUCING NEW CONCEPTS

Introducing Count–Controlled Loops

These slides can be downloaded from the HIAS website https://computing.hias.hants.gov.uk/course/view.php?id=51.

Delivery

They are designed to be delivered to the whole class before pupils move on to using a count-controlled loop module of work such as

Toy Give Away

Regular 2d shapes

Dog Chase

They can also be delivered to a small group of pupils if they are working independently through resources in pairs.

Revision

If more than one count-controlled loop module is used, the slides could be used as a quick revision rather than an introduction

Format

Slides are provided in PDF and PowerPoint formats, and teachers who purchased the book are authorized to adapt the resources within their school or on closed learning platforms such as Seesaw, Google Classroom or Teams, as long as they are not shared outside the school community.

Hints

Extra hints and tips on usage are provided alongside each slide on the following pages.

Resources

Pupils will need whiteboards and pens or paper and pencils

Knowledge Sheet

These is a knowledge sheet on page 11 that pupils can use to write their algorithms on and be reminded about key ideas.

Programming Ideas Simplified

Count Controlled Loops

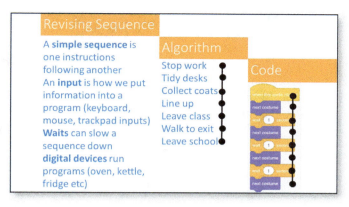

This slide reminds pupils of what they learnt about sequences in Year 3. Read the main points and point out sequence programming and sequence algorithms.

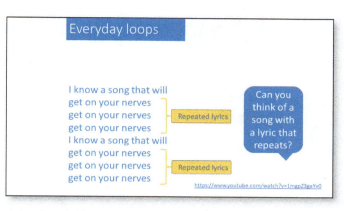

Ask a few children to sing or say popular repeated song lyrics.

Ask pupils to watch the dance video and dance any move that includes repetition until you spot them doing it, at which time they can look for another example of repetition.

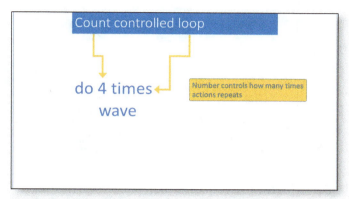

Explain that the number controls how many times wave repeats.

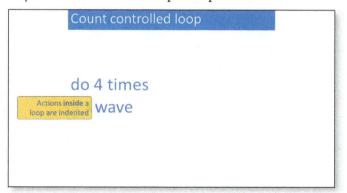

Point out that the wave is indented to show that it is inside the loop. All actions inside the loop are indented.

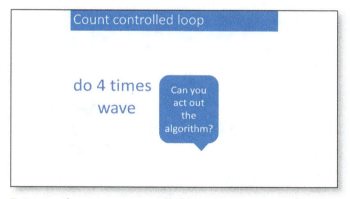

Point out that a count-controlled loop is a sequence of actions like wave, wave, wave, wave written in a different way.

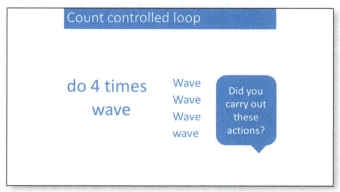

Watch your pupils carefully to see which ones are copying other children rather than following the instructions. When pupils are writing their own algorithms later, test these pupils with your own simple algorithm.

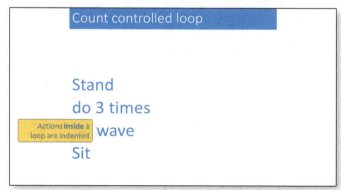

Point out that sit is not in the loop, as it is not indented.

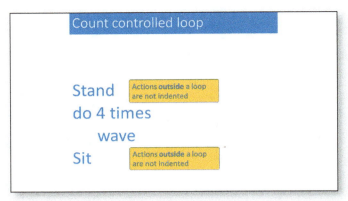

Point out that stand and sit are not in the loop, as they are not indented.

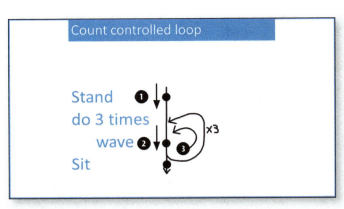

Trace your finger over the flow of control line while saying the actions. Now ask how we know that the loop repeats three times? Answer 3x symbol.

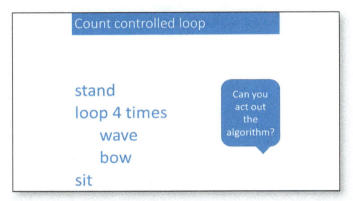

Watch carefully to see which pupils include sit inside the loop. If any pupils include sit inside the loop, point out that it is not indented.

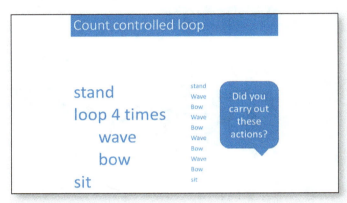

(The list helps pupils to see that a count controlled loop can be converted into a simple sequence very easily.)

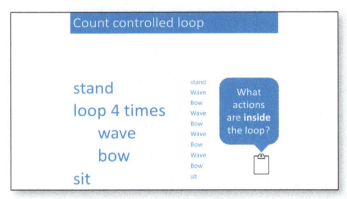

Ask pupils to answer this on a whiteboard.

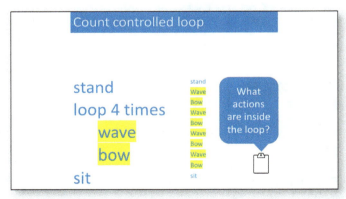

Point to both the actions inside the loop and those in the sequence highlighted in yellow.

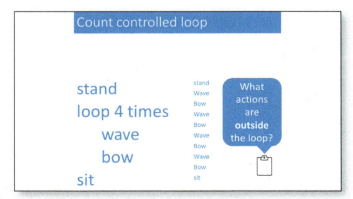

Ask pupils to answer this on a whiteboard.

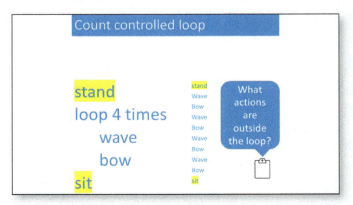

Point to both the actions inside the loop and those in the sequence highlighted in yellow.

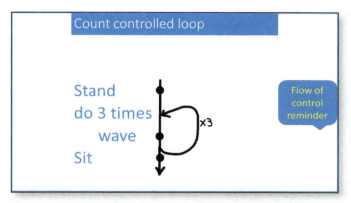

Point out that this is just an example to help them draw the next one themselves.

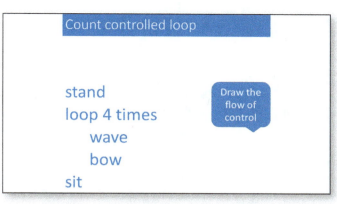

Remind pupils that they will need a dot for every action. Some pupils will benefit from this slide being printed out beforehand to be drawn on.

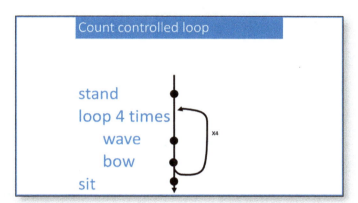

Break the flow diagram into parts and give marks for the sit dot, marks for the loop line, marks for wave and bow on the count-controlled loop and marks for stand at the top.

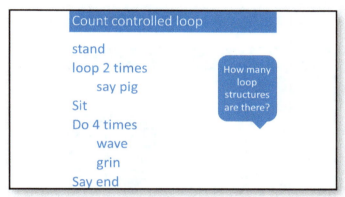

The loop structure is the part that tells you it is a loop.

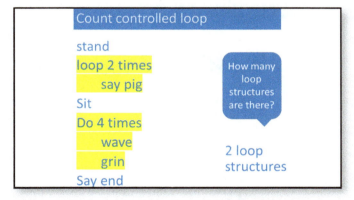

There are two loop structures, loop 2 times and do 4 times.

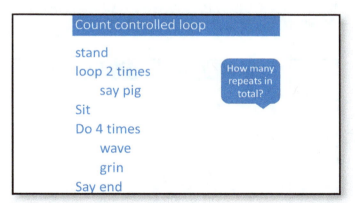

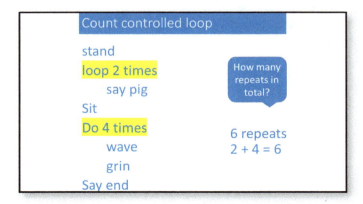

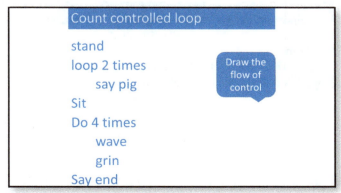

Some pupils will benefit from having this slide printed out to draw the flow directly on.

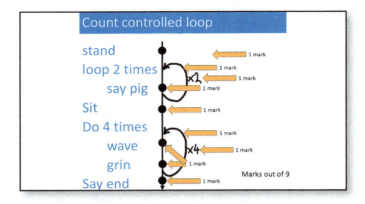

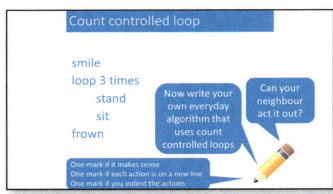

Pupils writing their own count-controlled loop algorithms that their partner can act out gives you time to formatively assess those who are struggling or provide writing or scribing support for those who you spotted in the earlier parts of the introduction.

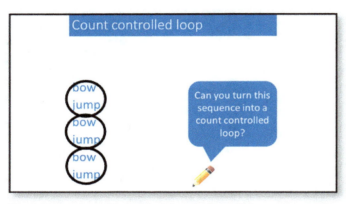

If pupils are struggling with this, ask them if they can spot the pattern in the sequence? Put circles around the pairs as shown. Ask pupils how many times the pattern is repeated.

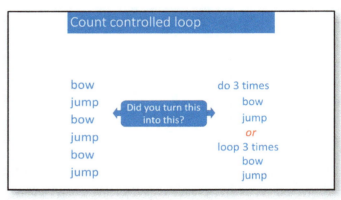

Point out that an algorithm can be written in any way as long as it can be understood by another human.
They could have used repeat 3 times.

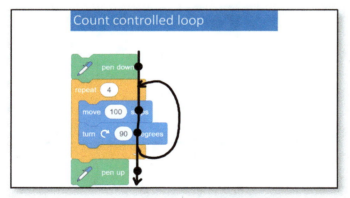

It is important to now point out what a count-controlled loop looks like in code. Identify that is called a repeat loop and point out where the number is.
Point out that the flow of control works on code count-controlled loops as it does on everyday algorithm count-controlled loops.

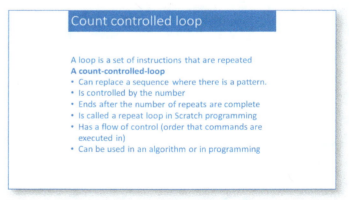

Read out this summary of the main points learnt from these slides.

Introducing Indefinite Loops

These slides can be downloaded from the HIAS website https://computing.hias.hants.gov.uk/course/view.php?id=51.

Delivery

They are designed to be delivered to the whole class before pupils move on to using indefinite loop modules of work such as

Fish Tank

Helicopter Game

They can also be delivered to a small group of pupils if they are working independently through resources in pairs.

Revision

If more than one indefinite loop module is used, the slides could be used as a quick revision rather than an introduction.

Format

Slides are provided in PDF and PowerPoint formats, and teachers who purchased the book are authorised to adapt the resources within their school or on closed learning platforms such as Seesaw, Google Classroom or Teams, as long as they are not shared outside the school community.

Hints

Extra hints and tips on usage are provided alongside each slide on the following pages.

Resources

Pupils will need whiteboards and pens or paper and pencils.

Knowledge Sheet

There is a knowledge sheet on page 11 that pupils can use to write their algorithms on and be reminded about key knowledge.

Programming Ideas Simplified

Indefinite infinite Loops

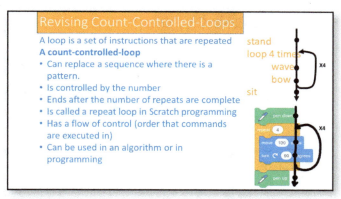

This is a revision slide to remind pupils of prior learning. (You will also find that sequence knowledge from Year 3 and revision questions are included in work on indefinite loops.)

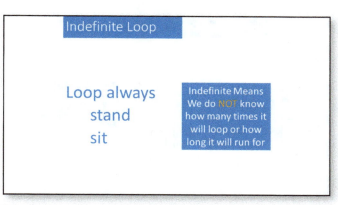

It is also sometimes called an infinite loop.

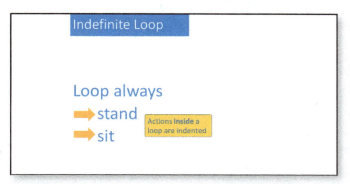

Actions inside a loop are indented just like they were in the count controlled loop. We have drawn arrows to remind you where the indents are.

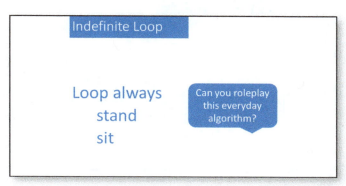

Can you roleplay this loop? After 20 seconds, ask the class to stop. Make the point that some pupils looped quickly and some were slow, and that you were not sure how many repetitions they would go through.

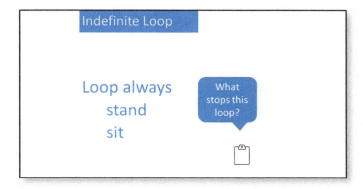

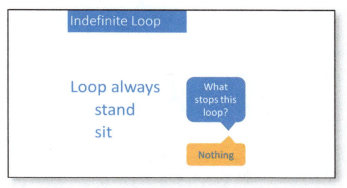

In algorithm form acted out by a human, only tiredness or being bored would stop the loop. As programming in a digital device only pulling the plug would stop this type of loop.

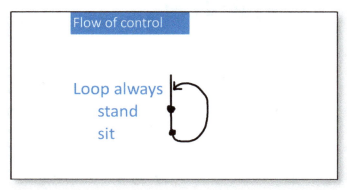

The flow of control is almost the same as a count-controlled loop, except that it never ends and we can't write a number next to the loop.

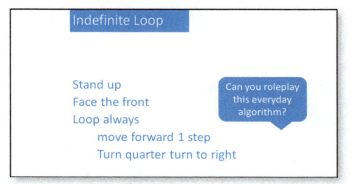

Can they roleplay the algorithm?

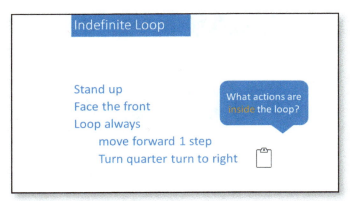

What actions are inside the loop?

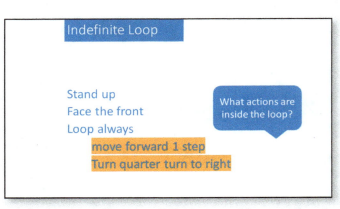

Move and turn and we can tell this because they are indented.

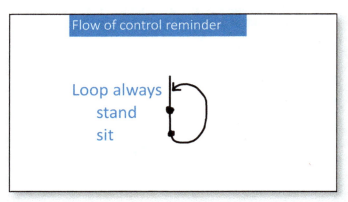

What actions are outside the loop?

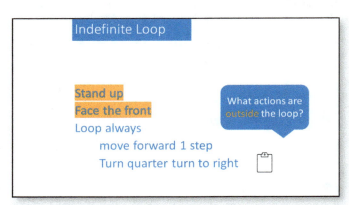

Stand up and face the front and we can tell this because they are not indented. Loop always is a loop structure not an action.

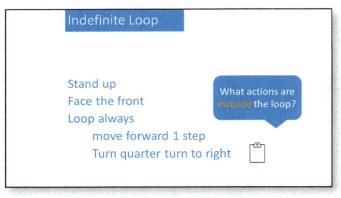

Here is a reminder of the flow of control. With the loop arrow coming back into the loop always and the actions shown as dots on the line.

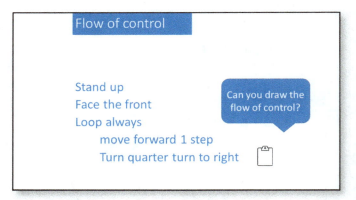

Now draw the flow of control on your whiteboards.

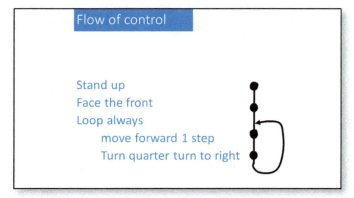

Well done, 1 mark if you got the two dots before the loop. One mark for two dots inside the loop. 1 mark for drawing the loop an making the arrow come back to loop always.

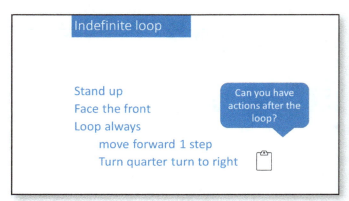

Can you have actions after the loop as we did with the count-controlled loop?

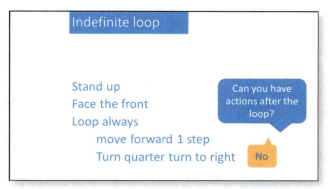

As an algorithm, we could write actions, but they would never be acted on. So no we can't have actions after an infinite indefinite loop. *(Later on they will find that some indefinite loops can be ended by conditions)*

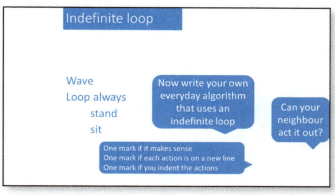

Can they write their own indefinite loops that their partner can act out. 1 mark if it makes sense. 1 mark if actions inside the loop are indented. 1 mark if each action is on a new line. Go round and check that pupils have completed this. Scribe for any pupil that needs it.

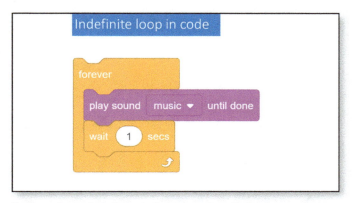

In Scratch, an indefinite infinite loop is called a forever loop.

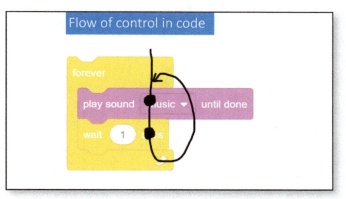

We can draw the flow of control on an infinite indefinite loop in the same way.

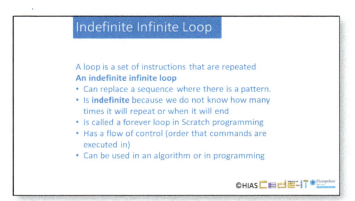

Now read through a summary of the knowledge learnt in these slides.

PROGRAMMING MODULES THAT USE COUNT-CONTROLLED LOOPS

CHAPTER 3   Toy Give Away

> **Overview**
> Pupils explore how Scratch can make objects move and transform using count-controlled loops before programming their own objects using count-controlled loops.

To do before the session

1. Look at the grid below and decide which optional and SEN activities you are going to include and exclude.
2. Print pupil worksheets for each activity chosen and staple into a booklet, one for each pupil.
3. Print marksheets for activities chosen to be placed where pupils can access them.
4. Download the code needed and place in a templates folder on your school network or add to a Scratch Studio or link on your learning platform.
5. Download the slides that go with the concept introduction.
6. Study the notes that go with the slides
7. Examine the teacher help notes that are provided alongside every activity.

To do at the start of the session

If you have not introduced count-controlled loops with this class before, do this first as a whole class activity.

To do after the concept has been introduced

Each activity has whole class notes to help you explain what is needed if it is the first time pupils have carried out this type of activity. There are also core instructions underneath in case you are sticking to the core activities only.

How this module fits into a programming progression

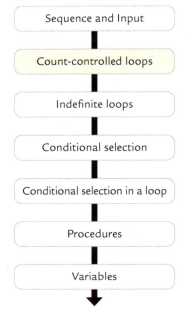

Sequence and Input

Count-controlled loops

Indefinite loops

Conditional selection

Conditional selection in a loop

Procedures

Variables

> **Vocabulary**
> Count-controlled loop, loop, repeat, do x times. Sprite, costume, backdrop, position, motion, degrees, direction, keyboard,

Resource Name	Core Optional SEN	Teacher	Pupil Grouping	How Assessed	SCRATCH ACCESS
CONCEPT Count-controlled loop (page)	CORE	Leads Session	Solo whole class activity	Formative	NO
PARSONS	OPTIONAL SEN OPTIONAL ALL **(predict or Parsons, not both)**	Support Poor Readers	Solo or Paired (Teacher choice)	Pupil Marked Marksheet Provided	YES Toygiveway Parsons
PREDICT	OPTIONAL ALL **(predict or Parsons, not both)**	Support Poor Readers	Paired	Pupil Marked Marksheet Provided	NO
INVESTIGATE	CORE	Support Poor Readers	Paired	Pupil Marked Marksheet Provided	YES Toygiveaway
FLOW	OPTIONAL ALL OPTIONAL ABLE	Support Poor Readers	Solo or Paired (Teacher Choice)	Pupil Marked Marksheet Provided	NO
CHANGE	CORE	Support Poor Readers	Paired	Pupil Marked Marksheet Provided	YES Toygiveaway
CREATE	CORE	Assesses pupil work and checks pupil self-assessment	Solo	Pupil Assessed & Teacher Assessed	YES Toygiveaway

24   (Yellow is core module, pink and white are optional.)

Core activities general instructions

1. Group pupils in roughly same ability pairs. For **investigate** and **change** worksheets pupils will work in pairs, for **create** they will work separately.

2. Give out the pupil booklets and explain that pupils need to follow the instructions on the sheets to explore how **count-controlled loops** work.

3. Explain that each pupil will record separately while working alongside their partner and keeping to the same pace as their partner.

4. Demonstrate where they can find the template code and explain that pupils will share one device for investigate and change.

5. Explain that during each question, only one person should touch the shared device and they should swap who that person is when there is a new questions.

6. Encourage them to discuss their answers with their partner. If they disagree with their partner, they can record a different answer in their own booklet.

7. Show pupils where it says they should mark their work on the sheet and where the answer sheets are in the classroom.

8. Remind pupils to return marksheets after marking, because there are not enough for every pair to have their own.

Key programming knowledge

A loop is any set of instructions that are repeated

An algorithm is any set of instructions to carry out a task that can be understood by another human

A count-controlled loop

Can replace a sequence where there is a pattern.

Is controlled by the number

Ends after the number of repeats are complete

Is called a repeat loop in Scratch programming

Has a flow of control (order that commands are executed in)

Can be used in an algorithm or in programming

Resources

Toygiveaway	https://scratch.mit.edu/projects/318201426
Toygiveawayparsons	https://scratch.mit.edu/projects/324776240/

	On the sheet, if it says no Scratch, they must work only on the sheet.
	If it says Scratch with a green tick, they can use one device between the pair.
	If it says work with a partner, they must work at the same speed as their partner.
	If it says work on their own, they must do this using a separate device, each working alone.

The First Software Loop

The scholarly consensus is that the first instance of a software loop was the loop **Ada Lovelace** used to calculate Bernoulli numbers using **Charles Babbage**'s Analytical Engine mechanical computer.

Scottish Curriculum for Excellence Technologies

I understand the instructions of a visual programming language and can predict the outcome of a program written using the language. TCH 1-14a

I can explain core programming language concepts in appropriate technical language. TCH 2-14a

I can demonstrate a range of basic problem solving skills by building simple programs to carry out a given task, using an appropriate language. TCH 1-15a

I can create, develop and evaluate computing solutions in response to a design challenge. TCH 2-15a

English Computing National Curriculum Programs of Study

Pupils should be taught to:

- **design, write and debug programs that accomplish specific goals**, including controlling or simulating physical systems; solve problems by decomposing them into smaller parts.

- **use sequence**, selection and **repetition in programs**; work with variables **and various forms of input and output**.

- **use logical reasoning to explain how some simple algorithms work and to detect and correct errors in algorithms and programs.**

Welsh National Curriculum Relevant Strands

Progression Step 3.

- I can identify repeating patterns and use loops to make my algorithms more concise.
- I can explain and debug algorithms.

Toy Give Away PARSONS

Start Scratch and load
toy give away parsons

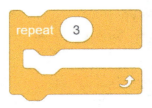

Count-Controlled Loop

All the code has been selected but some of it in the app is unconnected.

Use the algorithms below to help you connect the code.

Beachball	Balloon	Bowtie
Start when touched	Start when touched	Start when touched
Go to a specific x and y place	Go to a specific x and y place	Set size to 160%
Point up	Start on costume 1a	Go to a specific x and y place
Loop 4 times	Loop 3 times	Point right
Move 20 steps forward	Change costume	Make bigger by set size to 240%
Pause	Pause	Loop 100 times
Move 20 steps backwards		Turn right 15°
Pause		Point right
		Make smaller by set size to 160°
Beachball	Balloon	Bowtie

Now check your answers to see if they are correct using the Parsons marksheet

Supporting Parsons

Whole class advice

Load toygiveawayparsons code and then use the algorithm on this page to build the code. When you have completed it, run the code and check your answer with the marking sheet.

Able advice

Parsons problems can be made more complex by separating more blocks in the example Scratch code and saving that version as a new template.

Send advice

Parsons problems can be made less complex by connecting more blocks in the example Scratch code and saving that version as a new template.

Notes on the activity

This allows pupils to build part of the code first before investigating, modifying and creating code of their own. The algorithm is written in language similar but also different to the code. This helps pupils by enabling them to see an example of planning which will help them when they come to plan their own project. On its own, it is not enough deep thinking about the code to enable agency, but as a starter or SEN activity it is useful to see how code can be built.

Understanding programming

You can find out more about Parsons problems in the teacher book, Chapter 19.

Individual advice

Pointing out that the code inside a loop is indented can help some pupils.

All the code has been selected but some of it in the app is unconnected. Use the algorithms below to help you connect the code.

Beachball	Balloon	Bowtie
		Start when touched
Start when touched	Start when touched	Set size to 160%
Go to a specific x and y place	Go to a specific x and y place	Go to a specific x and y place
Point up	Start on costume 1a	Point right
Loop 4 times	Loop 3 times	Make bigger by set size to 240%
Move 20 steps forward	Change costume	Loop 100 times
Pause	Pause	Turn right 15°
Move 20 steps backwards		Point right
Pause		Make smaller by set size to 160°

Beachball

Balloon

Bowtie

Toy Give Away PREDICT

Don't load Scratch
Work with a partner

Work with a partner

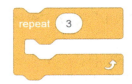

Count-Controlled Loop

Beachball

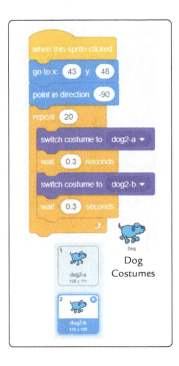

Dog
Costumes

Bowtie

Bells

Reading Code

1. How **many** repeat loops (count-controlled loops) can you spot on this **page**?

    _____

2. Put a **tick** by the loop which repeats the **most**?
3. Put a **cross** by the loop which repeats the **least**?
4. Which toy does **not** have a wait inside the loop?

    _____

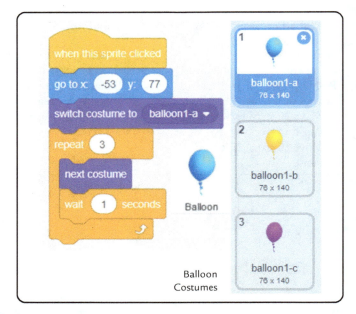

Balloon

Balloon
Costumes

Predicting

Read the code carefully with your partner. Start with the beachball. Focus on what is inside the repeat loop. What do you predict the toys will **do** when the code is run? Tick the correct prediction

Beachball	Balloon	Bowtie	Bells	Dog
I think the beachball will	I think the balloon will	I think the bowtie will	I think the bells will	I think the dog will
☐ roll side to side	☐ change colours	☐ bounce up and down	☐ spin	☐ spin round
☐ bounce up and down	☐ float off	☐ spin round	☑ Swing from side to side	☐ wiggle its legs
☐ spin around	☐ pop	☐ disappear	☐ disappear	☐ bounce
☐ roll off the page	☐ spin round	☐ flash on the screen	☐ Fall off table	☐ hide and show

photocopiable page

A

Supporting PREDICT

Whole class advice

Make sure you work with your partner on this sheet. Take it in turns to read a section and tell your partner what you think it does. Then answer the questions using your understanding of the code.

Can you see the blue go to x and y blocks? These blocks make the toy go to the same place on the screen every time it is clicked.

Notes on the activity

This optional activity helps pupils to think about the bigger purpose of the program before they start looking at parts of it in later sections.

Send advice

Support pairs of pupils who are poor readers by reading questions, reading code samples and covering up questions until they get to them.

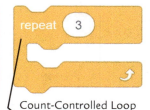

Count-Controlled Loop

Remember a count-controlled loop is called a repeat loop in Scratch. There is even a block in the top right corner to remind you.

Focus on what is inside the count-controlled loop. Remember this is called a repeat loop in Scratch.

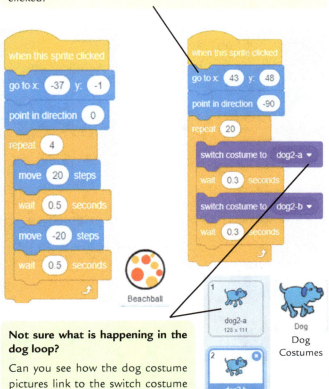

Beachball

Dog

dog2-a
128 x 111

dog2-b
128 x 105

Dog Costumes

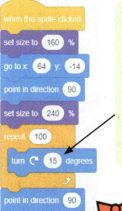

Bowtie

Not sure what is happening in a specific loop?

Draw or trace the flow of control, or part of it if it is a high number loop. Say the actions in the order they happen.

Not sure what is happening in the balloon loop?

If it starts on balloon1-a what costume do you think next costume will change it to? What will that look like? Go through the flow of control.

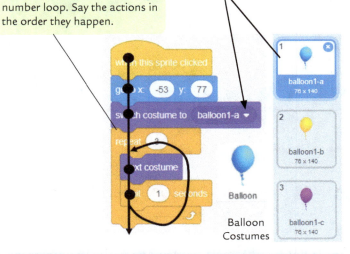

Balloon

balloon1-a
76 x 140

balloon1-b
76 x 140

balloon1-c
76 x 140

Balloon Costumes

Not sure what is happening in the dog loop?

Can you see how the dog costume pictures link to the switch costume commands in the code?

Reading Code (answers in red)

1. How **many** repeat loops (count controlled loops) can you spot on this **page**?

   5 or 6 if you include the picture in the top right hand side.

2. Put a **tick** by the loop which repeats the **most**? Bowtie.

3. Put a **cross** by the loop which repeats the **least**? Balloon.

4. Which toy does **not** have a wait inside the loop? Bowtie.

Predicting

Beachball	Balloon	Bowtie	Bells	Dog
I think the beachball will	I think the balloon will	I think the bowtie will	I think the bells will	I think the dog will
☐ roll side to side	☐ change colours (1 mark)	☐ bounce up and down	☐ spin	☐ spin round
☐ bounce up and down (1 mark)	☐ float off	☐ spin round (1 mark)	☑ Swing from side to side	☐ wiggle its legs (1 mark)
☐ spin around	☐ pop	☐ disappear	☐ disappear	☐ bounce
☐ roll off the page	☐ spin round	☐ flash on the screen	☐ Fall off table	☐ hide and show

If a pupil doesn't want to predict in case they are wrong

Say that you learn a lot from getting a prediction wrong. I am always really impressed when pupil try even when they are not sure if they are right or wrong.

Toy Give Away
INVESTIGATE

Don't load
Scratch

Work with a partner

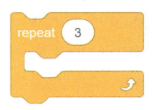

repeat   3

Count-Controlled Loop

Start Scratch and load the
Toy give away program

Play toy give away a few times. A green flag starting
block will introduce the app. Click on each toy to run
their code.

Mark your reading code and predicting what it will do questions from the last sheet.

Investigate the Code

Run the programs lots of times to help you answer the questions but don't change the code

Look at the code inside the **balloon** sprite.

Balloon

1. When the balloon sprite is clicked, how many times will next costume be run? _____

2. How long is there between each costume change? _____

3. Circle the sequence that could replace the balloon loop and still keep the same balloon colour changing effect.

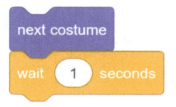

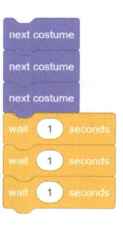

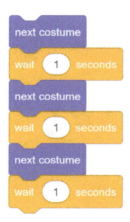

Look at the code inside the **bowtie** and answer these questions.

Bowtie

4. Which direction is the bowtie pointing before it spins?
    (number of degrees) _____

5. What is the largest percentage % the bowtie grows to? _____

Look at the code inside the **beachball** and answer these questions.

Beachball

6. When the sprite is clicked how many times does it wait for
    0.5 seconds? _____ (2, 4, 8 or 16)

7. What direction does –20 move the ball? _____ (up or down)

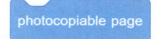

photocopiable page

Now mark the investigate questions using the answer sheet

Supporting INVESTIGATE

Whole class advice

Work in pairs, one device between the pair. Take it in turns every question to swap who runs code. You must work at the same pace as your partner and not move on to the next question until you have both written your answer down. If you disagree, write a different answer. You must mark your work before moving on to the next section.

Notes on the activity

Investigating the code encourages pupils to think deeply about how it works. Check that every pupil is filling in and marking the questions individually but at the pace of the slowest in the pair. Sometimes a pair decides not to mark to speed up their efforts. Marking gives valuable information so I recommend sending them back to mark their work. A class instruction to come and talk to you if they have over half of the questions wrong or they do not understand the answer after they have marked it helps to check progress is being made correctly. There is real value in collecting these scores to build up a summative picture of pupil progress.

Are they looking in the correct sprite?

Lots of avoidable mistakes are made by looking at the wrong code.

Send advice

Support pairs of pupils who are poor readers by reading questions, reading code samples and covering up questions until they get to them.

Run the Code

Play toy give away a few times. A green flag starting block will introduce the app. Click on each toy to run their code.

Did you predict the outcomes?

Mark your reading code and predicting what it will do questions using the answer sheet.

Q1 HINT Point out where next costume is in the code, ask them what type of loop is it inside?

Walk away at this point, as that is enough of a hint.

Investigate the Code

Run the programs lots of times to help you answer the questions but don't change the code.

Balloon

Q3 Count-controlled loops can always be changed into sequences, although only sequences with patterns are suitable for changing into count-controlled loops.

Look at the code inside the **balloon** sprite.

1. When the balloon sprite is clicked, how **many times** will next costume be run?

   3 times (1 mark)

2. How long is there between each costume change?

   1 second (1 mark)

3. Circle the sequence that could replace the balloon loop and still keep the same balloon colour changing effect.

 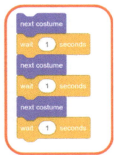

Q3 HINT Rephrase the question. Run the code and watch what it does. Which of these sequences could replace the repeat loop and the code that gets repeated?

Q4 HINT Which part of the code does the spinning? Wait until they have identified the loop. What directions are before the spin/loop?

Look at the code inside the **bowtie** and answer these questions.

Bowtie

4. Which direction is the bowtie pointing before it spins? (number of degrees)

   90 degrees or pointing right (1 mark for either)

5. What is the largest percentage % the bowtie grows to?

   240% (1 mark)

Q6 HINT How many wait blocks are there in the loop?

Wait until they say the answer 2

How many times are both those wait blocks going to be repeated? Walk away.

Look at the code inside the **beachball** and answer these questions.

Beachball

6. When the sprite is clicked how many times does it wait for 0.5 seconds?

   8 times (1 mark) (2, 4, 8 or 16)

7. What direction does −20 move the ball?

   Down (1 mark) (up or down)

Q7 HINT Does move 20 or move −20 come first in the loop? Run the code, what does it do first?

31

TOY GIVE AWAY

FLOW

Work on
your own

1. Circle the correct flow of control diagram.

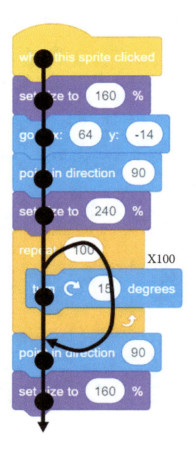
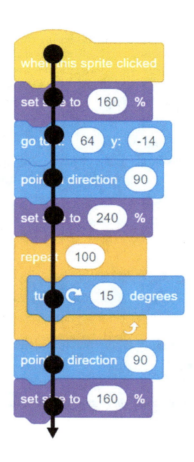
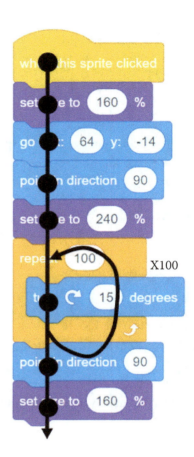

X100

X100

Say if these statements are TRUE or FALSE

2. A repeat loop **IS** a count-controlled loop _____

3. A count-controlled loop is called a repeat loop in Scratch _____

4. A count-controlled loop will always have an end _____

5. You can only put one action inside a
    count-controlled loop _____

6. Draw the flow of control on
    This code.

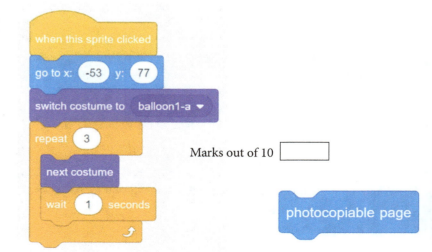

Marks out of 10 [   ]

photocopiable page

32

SUPPORTING FLOW

Work on
your own

Teacher notes on this activity

This could be completed in a test environment or carried out as the last activity. It should never replace the programming create challenge. The national curriculum stipulates that pupils should be able to use repetition in programs. As a way of determining how much has been learnt about count-controlled loops, it is a useful assessment addition.

Whole class advice

Work on your own without using Scratch to answer these questions about the flow of control. Make sure you mark this work when you have finished.

1. Circle the correct flow of control diagram.

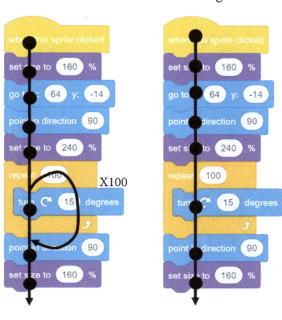

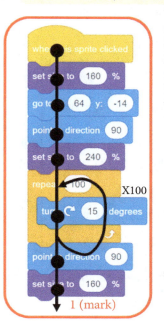

1 (mark)

Send able advice

Support pupils who are poor readers by reading questions, reading code samples and covering up questions until they get to them.

Notes

Few supportive notes are provided with this activity as it is an independent assessment.

Say if these statements are TRUE or FALSE

2. A repeat loop **IS** a count-controlled loop TRUE (1 mark).

3. A count-controlled loop is called a repeat loop in Scratch TRUE (1 mark).

4. A count-controlled loop will always have an end TRUE (1 mark).

5. You can only put one action inside a count-controlled loop FALSE (1 mark).

6. Draw the flow of control on This code.

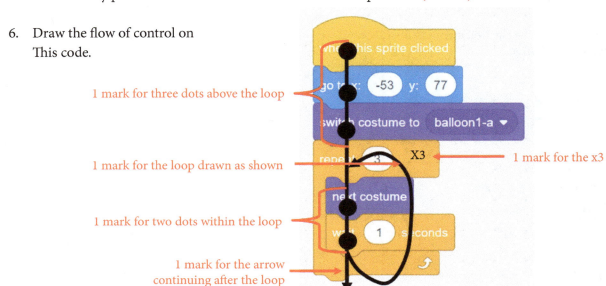

1 mark for three dots above the loop

1 mark for the loop drawn as shown

1 mark for two dots within the loop

1 mark for the arrow continuing after the loop

1 mark for the x3

Toy Give Away
CHANGE

Start Scratch and load the
Toy give away program

Work with a partner

Count-Controlled Loop

Make small changes to the code.

1. Change the code to make the **dog** walk slower.
    Describe what you changed.

Dog

2. Change the code to make the beachball bounce higher.
    Describe what you changed.

Beachball

3. Change the code to make the bowtie spin slower.
    Describe what you changed.

Bowtie

4. Change the code to make the balloon change through
    all the colours twice. Describe what you changed.

Balloon

5. Change the code to make the **bell** swing in a wider arc.
    Describe what you changed.

Bells

What is an arc?

If we swung a piece of string
from the blue circle, how far it
swings would be the arc.

photocopiable page

Now mark the changing code questions using the answer sheet.

Supporting CHANGE

Whole class advice

Work in pairs, one device between the pair. Take it in turns every question to swap who runs code. You must work at the same pace as your partner and not move on to the next question until you have both written your answer down. If you disagree, write a different answer. You must mark your work before moving on to the next section.

Q2 The simple answer to this is to change move 20 steps to a larger number. Technically pupils should change both move 20 steps and move −20 steps to the same number one positive and one negative so the ball returns to bounce on the same part of the table. To stretch a pupil, ask them how they can also get the ball to bounce higher but bounce on the same spot on the table.

Make small changes to the code.

1. Change the code to make the **dog** walk slower. Describe what you changed.

   Increase both waits to numbers larger than 0.3 (1 mark)

   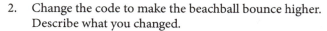
   Dog

2. Change the code to make the beachball bounce higher. Describe what you changed.

   Change the move 20 steps to a higher number (1 mark)

   Beachball

3. Change the code to make the bowtie spin slower. Describe what you changed.

   Reduce the amount of turn to less than 15 degrees (1 mark)

   Bowtie

4. Change the code to make the balloon change through all the colours twice. Describe what you changed.

   Increase the number of repeats to 6 (1 mark)

   Balloon

5. Change the code to make the **bell** swing in a wider arc. Describe what you changed.

   Change the turn right and turn left degrees to numbers larger than 20 (1 mark)

   Bells

Now mark the change the code questions using the answer sheet.

Whole class advice

Cross out the last question for pupils who work at a slower pace than their peers so they get to create code.

If we swung a piece of string from the blue circle, how far it swings would be the arc.

Notes on the activity

Changing or modifying code is a core part of this module, so I suggest you do not leave it out. It is an important step towards creation of their own code as parts they have modified they will feel more ownership of. Recording marks will help with assessment.

Send able advice

Support pairs of pupils who are poor readers by reading questions, reading code samples and covering up questions until they get to them.

Are they looking in the correct sprite?

Lots of avoidable mistakes are made by looking at the wrong code.

Q1 Ask pupils to underline key words in the question. Hopefully when they underline slower you can say that slower is a time word and that they should look for time words in the code.

This hints that they should look for the wait block but don't say that

Tracing the flow of control would also help with this.

Q3 Ask pupils what makes the bowtie spin inside the loop? As there is only one block inside the loop, it hints that the degrees need changing.

Q4 Ask pupils how many colours does the balloon change to? Answer 3 Then ask are any colour repeated? Answer no. Then ask How can you get all three colour to repeat twice?

Q5 If pupils are stuck here, it is often about the arc language. Point them to the explanation at the bottom and demonstrate an arc using a pencil or ruler.

Have they marked this worksheet?

Check that they have marked it and take in the results to inform assessment.

Toy Give Away App
CREATE

Work on
your own

Count-Controlled Loop

Make first

Add another toy sprite to the table and program it using a repeat (count-controlled) loop. You can adapt one of the ideas from toy give away such as moving up-down, rotating, changing costumes, playing a sound, etc.

Make second

Plan your own scene with sprites that do something when they are clicked. You must use count-controlled loops as part of some sprites programming.

My Program Idea

Draw your scene. What will your sprites do?

Teacher & Pupil Assessment

Circle one column on each row to show what you think you have achieved

	Not used a count control loop	Copied a count control loop from the toy give away project	Copied and changed a count control loop idea	Used a count control loop in a way not shown
Count controlled Loops	0 marks	1 mark	2 marks	3 marks

	Not used previous programming concepts for real purpose	Used previous programming concepts for real purpose
Used previous programming concept such as sequence and inputs	0 marks	1 mark

	No theme in planning or code	Has a theme in planning or code
(Only to be used if make second has been planned and created)		
Has a project theme in planning or code	0 marks	1 mark

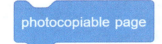

photocopiable page

Supporting CREATE

Notes on the activity

The make part of a project is really important and teachers should always make sure that pupils have time to make their own project, even if that means reducing the time spent on other stages for pupils who work slowly. It helps if pupils work on their own for this while supporting their partner.

Make first

Add another toy sprite to the table and program it using a repeat (count-controlled) loop. You can adapt one of the ideas from **toy give away** such as moving up-down, rotating, changing costumes, playing a sound, etc.

Send advice

Some pupils can really benefit from the teacher building a simple count-controlled loop at this point just so they can see how the blocks snap together.

Make second

Plan your own scene with sprites that do something when they are clicked. You must use count-controlled loops as part of some sprites programming.

Whole class advice

There is a foldable photocopiable card to remind pupils how to get extra sound and pen commands on page 46.

My Program Idea
A toy drum that plays a beat when touched

Draw your scene. What will your sprites do?

Touch to start
Repeat 10
   Drum beat
   Pause half second
   Say that is how to play the drum

This is a great opportunity to ask pupils questions about their code and factor that into your marking.

Where did you get that idea?

If it was an external source

Did you change it much?

Is it finished or is there more to add?

Encourage pupils to keep planning brief. Stick people, brief sketch, simple algorithm.

Modelling a plan can be helpful to many pupils. With that in mind this is a simple plan you can use or adapt on the left.

Ask pupils to assess their own programming using the assessment grid below. You can use this as a basis for a discussion about things they can improve.

Teacher assessment

Circle one column on each row to show what you think you have achieved

	Not used a count control loop	Copied a count control loop from the toy give away project	Copied and changed a count control loop idea	Used a count control loop in a way not shown
Count controlled Loops	0 marks	1 mark	2 marks	3 marks

	Not used previous programming concepts for real purpose	Used previous programming concepts for real purpose
Used previous programming concept such as sequence and inputs	0 marks	1 mark

	No theme in planning or code	Has a theme in planning or code
(Only to be used if make second has been planned and created) **Has a project theme in planning or code**	0 marks	1 mark

Toy Give Away
Parsons MARKSHEET

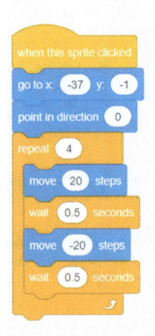

```
when this sprite clicked
go to x: -37 y: -1
point in direction 0
repeat 4
    move 20 steps
    wait 0.5 seconds
    move -20 steps
    wait 0.5 seconds
```

Beachball

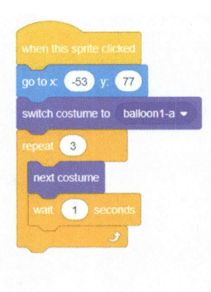

```
when this sprite clicked
go to x: -53 y: 77
switch costume to balloon1-a ▾
repeat 3
    next costume
    wait 1 seconds
```

Balloon

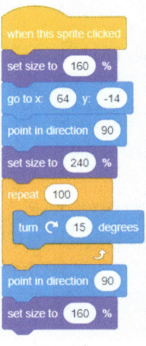

```
when this sprite clicked
set size to 160 %
go to x: 64 y: -14
point in direction 90
set size to 240 %
repeat 100
    turn ↻ 15 degrees
point in direction 90
set size to 160 %
```

Bowtie

photocopiable page

Toy Give Away
PREDICTING

Marksheet

Reading code

1. How **many** repeat loops (count controlled loops) can you spot on this **page**?

   5 or 6 if you include the picture in the top right hand side (1 mark)

2. Put a **tick** by the loop which repeats the most?

   Tick by the Bowtie loop (1 mark)

3. Put a **cross** by the loop which repeats the least?

   Tick by the Balloon loop (1 mark)

4. Which toy does not have a wait inside the loop?

   Bowtie (1 mark)

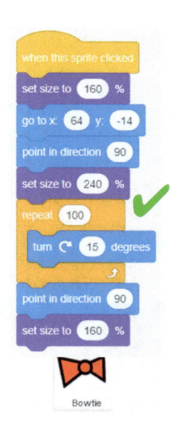

Bowtie

Balloon

Predicting

Beachball	Balloon	Bowtie	Bells	Dog
I think the beachball will	I think the balloon will	I think the bowtie will	I think the bells will	I think the dog will
☐ roll side to side	☑ change colours (1 mark)	☐ bounce up and down	☐ spin	☐ spin round
☑ bounce up and down (1 mark)	☐ float off	☑ spin round (1 mark)	☑ swing from side to side	☑ wiggle its legs (1 mark)
☐ spin around	☐ pop	☐ disappear	☐ disappear	☐ bounce
☐ roll off the page	☐ spin round	☐ flash on the screen	☐ Fall off table	☐ hide and show

Marks out of 8

photocopiable page

Toy Give Away
Investigating

Marking Sheet

Investigate the code
Look at the code inside the **balloon** sprite.

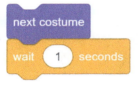

Balloon

1. When the balloon sprite is clicked, how many times will next costume be run?

    3 times (1 mark)

2. How long is there between each costume change?

    1 second (1 mark)

3. Circle the sequence that could replace the balloon loop and still keep the same balloon colour changing effect.

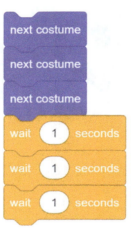
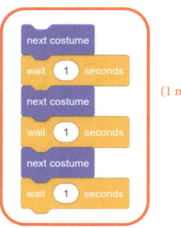

(1 mark)

Look at the code inside the **bowtie** and answer these questions.

Bowtie

4. Which direction is the bowtie pointing before it spins? (number of degrees)

    90 degrees or pointing right (1 mark for either)

5. What is the largest percentage % the bowtie grows to?

    240% (1 mark)

Look at the code inside the **beachball** and answer these questions.

Beachball

6. When the sprite is clicked how many times does it wait for 0.5 seconds?

    8 times (1 mark)

7. What direction does –20 move the ball?

    Down (1 mark)

Marks out of 7

photocopiable page

F

FLOW MARKSHEET

1. Circle the correct flow of control diagram.

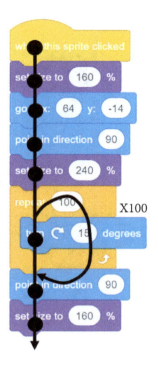

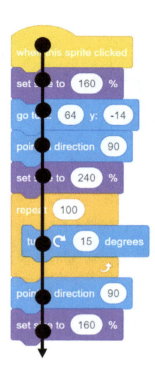

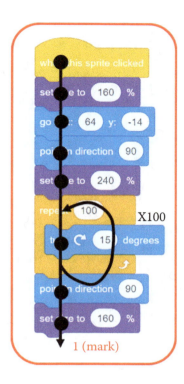

1 (mark)

Say if these statements are TRUE or FALSE

2. A repeat loop **IS** a count-controlled loop TRUE (1 mark).

3. A count-controlled loop is called a repeat loop in Scratch TRUE (1 mark).

4. A count-controlled loop will always have an end TRUE (1 mark).

5. You can only put one action inside a count-controlled loop FALSE (1 mark).

6. Draw the flow of control on
This code.

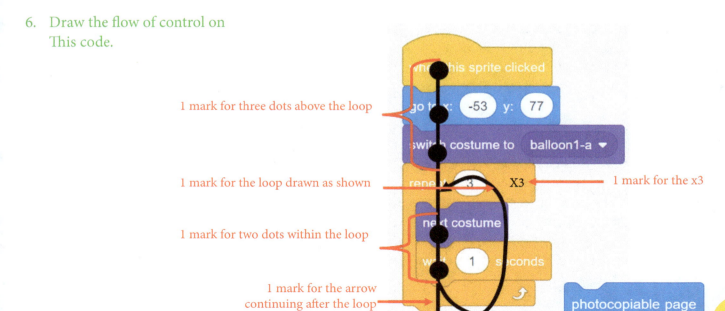

1 mark for three dots above the loop

1 mark for the loop drawn as shown

X3   1 mark for the x3

1 mark for two dots within the loop

1 mark for the arrow
continuing after the loop

photocopiable page

41

Toy Give Away
Changing

Marksheet

Make small changes to the code.

1. Change the code to make the **dog** walk slower. Describe what you changed and where you changed it.

    Increase both waits to numbers larger than 0.3 (1 mark)

Dog

2. Change the code to make the beachball bounce higher. Describe what you changed and where you changed it.

    Change the move 20 steps to a higher number (1 mark)

Beachball

3. Change the code to make the bowtie spin slower. Describe what you changed and where you changed it.

    Reduce the amount of turn to less than 15 degrees (1 mark)

Bowtie

4. Change the code to make the balloon change through all the colours twice. Describe you changed and where you changed it.

    Increase the number of repeats to 6 (1 mark)

Balloon

5. Change the code to make the **bell** swing in a wider arc. Describe what you changed and where you changed it.

    Change the turn right and turn left degrees to numbers larger than 20 (1 mark)

Bells

photocopiable page

Toy Give Away
CREATING

Marksheet

Make first

Add another toy sprite to the table and program it using a repeat (count-controlled) loop. You can adapt one of the ideas from **toy give away** such as moving up-down, rotating, changing costumes, playing a sound, etc.

Have you

- Added another toy sprite to the table.
- Program it using a repeat (count-controlled) loop.
- Adapted one of the ideas from toy give away such as moving up-down, rotating, changing costumes, playing a sound, etc.

Make second

Plan your own scene with sprites that do something when they are clicked. You must use count-controlled loops as part of some sprites programming.

> My Program Idea
>
> Have you added a program idea?

> Draw your scene. What will your sprites do?
>
>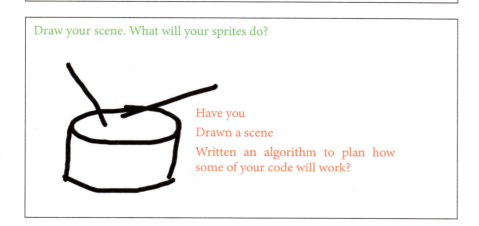
>
> Have you
>
> Drawn a scene
>
> Written an algorithm to plan how some of your code will work?

Teacher & Pupil Assessment

Circle one column on each row to show what you think you have achieved.

Have you used a count-controlled loop for 1-3 marks?	Not used a count-control loop	Copied a count-control loop from the toy give away project	Copied and changed a count-control loop idea	Used a count-control loop in a way not shown
Count-controlled Loops	0 marks	1 mark	2 marks	3 marks

	Not used previous programming concepts for real purpose	Used previous programming concepts for real purpose
Used previous programming concept such as sequence and inputs	0 marks	1 mark

(Only to be used if make second has been planned and created) Have you planned and created a theme?	No theme in planning or code	Has a theme in planning or code
Has a project theme in planning or code	0 marks	1 mark

Have you circle one column on each row to show what you think you have achieved?

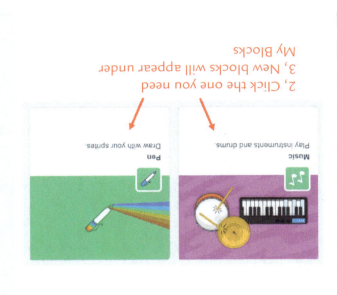

2, Click the one you need

3, New blocks will appear under My Blocks

Pen
Draw with your sprites.

Music
Play instruments and drums.

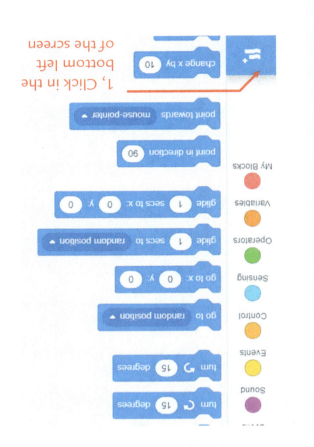

1, Click in the bottom left of the screen

My Blocks

Variables

Operators

Sensing

Control

Events

Sound

Adding pen or music blocks

Adding Pen or Music Blocks

photocopiable page

CHAPTER 4 — Exploring 2D Shapes

Overview

Pupils explore how Scratch can draw 2D shapes using count-controlled loops before drawing their own shapes and repeated patterns.

To do before the session

1. Look at the grid below and decide which optional and SEN activities you are going to include and exclude.

2. Print pupil worksheets for each activity chosen and staple into a booklet, one for each pupil.

3. Print marksheets for activities chosen to be placed where pupils can access them.

4. Download the code needed and place in a templates folder on your school network or add to a Scratch Studio or link on your learning platform.

5. Download the slides that go with the concept introduction.

6. Study the notes that go with the slides.

7. Examine the teacher help notes that are provided alongside every activity.

To do at the start of the session

If you have not introduced count-controlled loops with this class before do this first using the resources in Chapter 1 as a whole class activity.

To do after the concept has been introduced

Each activity has whole class notes to help you explain what is needed if it is the first time pupils have carried out this type of activity. There are also core instruction underneath in case you are sticking to the core activities only.

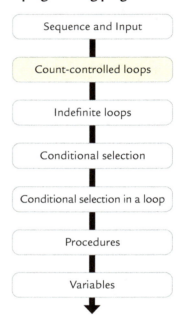

How this module fits into a programming progression

Sequence and Input

Count-controlled loops

Indefinite loops

Conditional selection

Conditional selection in a loop

Procedures

Variables

Vocabulary

Count-controlled loop, loop, repeat, do x times. Sprite, costume, backdrop, position, motion, degrees, direction, keyboard

Resource Name	Core Optional SEN	Teacher	Pupil Grouping	How Assessed	SCRATCH ACCESS
CONCEPT Count-controlled loop (page)	CORE	Leads Session	Solo whole class activity	Formative	NO
PARSONS	OPTIONAL SEN OPTIONAL ALL **Do predict or parsons not both**	Support Poor Readers	Solo or Paired (Teacher choice)	Pupil Marked Marksheet Provided	YES Exploring 2D shapes Parsons
PREDICT	OPTIONAL ALL **Do predict or parsons not both**	Support Poor Readers	Paired	Pupil Marked Marksheet Provided	NO
INVESTIGATE	CORE	Support Poor Readers	Paired	Pupil Marked Marksheet Provided	YES Exploring 2D shapes
FLOW	OPTIONAL SEN OPTIONAL ALL	Support Poor Readers	Solo or Paired (Teacher Choice)	Pupil Marked Marksheet Provided	NO
CHANGE	CORE	Support Poor Readers	Paired	Pupil Marked Marksheet Provided	YES Exploring 2D shapes
CREATE	CORE	Assesses pupil work and checks pupil self-assessment	Solo	Pupil Assessed & Teacher Assessed	YES Exploring 2D shapes

(Yellow is core module, pink and white are optional.)

Core activities general instructions

1. Group pupils in roughly same ability pairs. For **investigate** and **change** worksheets pupils will work in pairs, for **create** they will work separately.

2. Give out the pupil booklets and explain that pupils need to follow the instructions on the sheets to explore how **count-controlled loops** work.

3. Explain that each pupil will record separately while working alongside their partner and keeping to the same pace as their partner.

4. Demonstrate where they can find the template code and explain that pupils will share one device for investigate and change.

5. Explain that during each question only one person should touch the shared device and they should swap who that person is when there is a new questions.

6. Encourage them to discuss their answers with their partner. If they disagree with their partner, they can record a different answer in their own booklet.

7. Show pupils where it says they should mark their work on the sheet and where the answer sheets are in the classroom.

8. Remind pupils to return marksheets after marking, because there are not enough for every pair to have their own.

Key Programming Knowledge

A loop is any set of instructions that are repeated
An algorithm is any set of instructions to carry out a task that can be understood by another human

A count-controlled loop

Can replace a sequence where there is a pattern.

Is controlled by the number

Ends after the number of repeats are complete

Is called a repeat loop in Scratch programming

Has a flow of control (order that commands are run in)

Can be used in an algorithm or in programming

Resources

Exploring 2D shapes	https://scratch.mit.edu/projects/505515006/
Exploring 2D shapes parsons	https://scratch.mit.edu/projects/621357181/

 On the sheet, if it says no Scratch, they must work only on the sheet.

 If it says Scratch with a green tick, they can use one device between the pair.

 If it says work with a partner, they must work at the same speed as their partner.

 If it says work on their own, they must do this using a separate device each working alone.

The First Software Loop

The scholarly consensus is that the first instance of a software loop was the loop **Ada Lovelace** used to calculate Bernoulli numbers using **Charles Babbage's** Analytical Engine mechanical computer

Scottish Curriculum for Excellence Technologies

I understand the instructions of a visual programming language and can predict the outcome of a program written using the language. TCH 1-14a

I can explain core programming language concepts in appropriate technical language TCH 2-14a

I can demonstrate a range of basic problem solving skills by building simple programs to carry out a given task, using an appropriate language. TCH 1-15a

I can create, develop and evaluate computing solutions in response to a design challenge. TCH 2-15a

Welsh National Curriculum Relevant Strands

Progression Step 3.

♦ I can identify repeating patterns and use loops to make my algorithms more concise.

♦ I can explain and debug algorithms.

English Computing National Curriculum Programs of Study

Pupils should be taught to:

● **design, write and debug programs that accomplish specific goals**, including controlling or simulating physical systems; solve problems by decomposing them into smaller parts.

● **use sequence**, selection and **repetition in programs**; work with variables **and various forms of input and output**.

● **use logical reasoning to explain how some simple algorithms work and to detect and correct errors in algorithms and programs**

EXPLORING 2D SHAPES PARSONS

Start Scratch and load

EXPLORING 2D SHAPES PARSONS

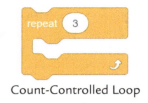

Count-Controlled Loop

All the code has been selected but some of it in the app is unconnected.

Use the algorithms below to help you connect the code.

Blue	Purple	Pink
A key starts	B key starts	C key starts
Erase lines	Erase lines	Erase lines
Blue pen	purple pen	pink pen
Pen size 1	Pen size 1	Pen size 6
Start drawing pen down	Start drawing pen down	Start drawing pen down
Loop 4 times	Loop 6 times	do 2 times
Move 40 steps forward	Move 45 steps forward	Move 120 steps forward
Pause 1 second	Pause half second	Turn left 90
Turn right 90	Turn left 60	Pause 1 second
Pause 1 second	Pause half second	Move 30 steps forward
Pen up stop drawing	Pen up stop drawing	Turn left 90
		Pause 1 second
		Pen up stop drawing

Now check your answers to see if they are correct using the Parsons marksheet.

SUPPORTING PARSONS

Whole class advice

Load **Exploring 2D Shapes Parsons** code and then use the algorithm on this page to build the code. When you have completed it, run the code and check your answer with the marking sheet.

Able advice

Parsons problems can be made more complex by separating more blocks in the example scratch code and saving that version as a new template. You can also remove the algorithm to make it much harder.

Send advice

Parsons problems can be made less complex by connecting more blocks in the example scratch code and saving that version as a new template.

Notes on the activity

This allows pupils to build part of the code first before investigating, modifying and creating code of their own. The algorithm is written in language similar but also different to the code. This helps pupils by enabling them to see an example of planning, which will help them when they come to plan their own project. On its own, it is not enough deep thinking about the code to enable agency but as a starter or SEN activity it is useful to see how code can be built.

Understanding programming

You can find out more about Parsons problems in the teacher book, Chapter 19.

Individual advice

Pointing out that the code inside a loop is indented can help some pupils.

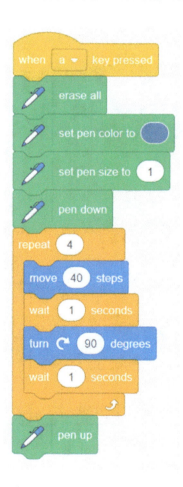
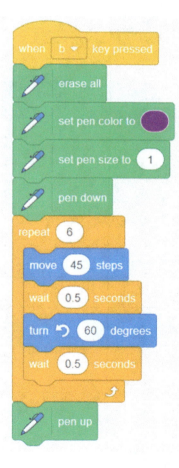
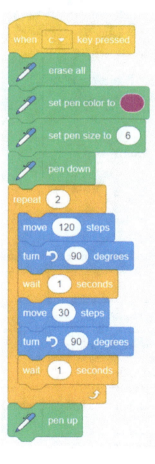

The correct answers

Exploring 2D Shapes
PREDICT

Work with a partner

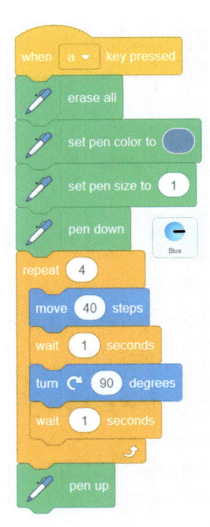
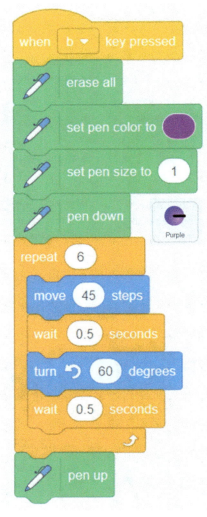
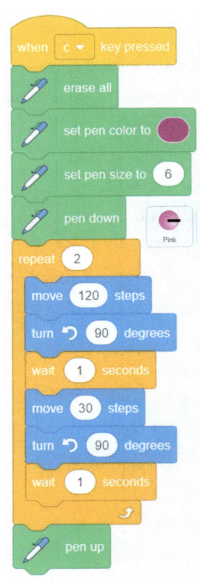

1. **Read the code carefully and complete the table**

	Blue Shape	Purple Shape	Pink Shape
Number of repeats		6	
Move steps number			120 and 30
Turn in degrees	90		

2. **Match the code with what it does**

Pen down on screen to start drawing	
Rub out all lines	
Make pen thickness 1	
Make line blue	

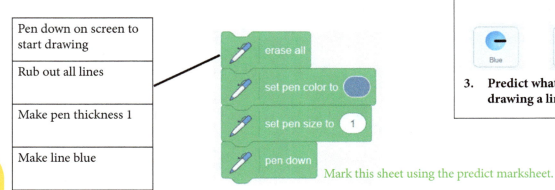

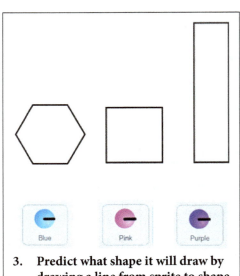

3. **Predict what shape it will draw by drawing a line from sprite to shape**

Mark this sheet using the predict marksheet.

photocopiable page

50

Supporting PREDICT

Notes on the activity

This optional activity helps pupils to think about the bigger purpose of the program before they start looking at parts of it in later sections.

Send advice

Support pairs of pupils who are poor readers by reading questions, reading code samples and covering up questions until they get to them.

Whole class advice

Make sure you work with your partner on this sheet. Take it in turns to read a section and tell your partner what you think it does. Then answer the questions using your understanding of the code.

Individal support

focus on what is inside the count-controlled loop. Say remember this is called a repeat loop in Scratch.

Q1 If pupils are struggling to complete the table, point them towards the loop parts of the code. Can they find where the numbers in the table are in code blocks? If they are still struggling, point one out.

Q3 If pupils are struggling to complete the prediction you can ask them to stand up and walk over the first example (blue) but only move 4 steps instead of 40. This quickly shows a square. You can do the same with the rectangle (pink) after reducing the steps to 12 and 3.

1. **Read the code carefully and complete the table**

	Blue Shape	Purple Shape	Pink Shape
Number of repeats	4	6	2
Move steps number	40	45	120 and 30
Turn in degrees	90	60	90

2. **Match the code with what it does**

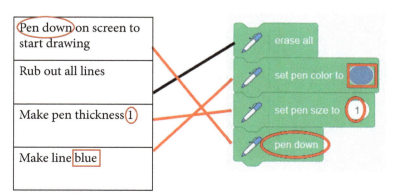

Q2 Word matching and number matching helps here.

3. **Predict what shape it will draw by drawing a line from sprite to shape**

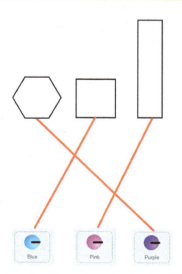

Exploring 2D Shapes
INVESTIGATE
Start Scratch and load Shape Loops

Don't load
Scratch

Work with a partner

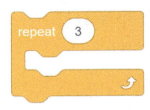

Count-Controlled Loop

Investigate the Code
Run the programs lot of times to help you answer the questions but do not change anything.
Run each shape a few times using the a, b, c, d and e keys.

Blue

Look at the code inside the blue sprite

1. How many times will **move 40 steps** be run?
   _____

2. How many times will **wait 1 seconds** be run?
   _____(2, 4 or 8)

Purple

Look at the code inside the purple sprite

3. How many times will **turn left 60 degrees** be run?
   _____

4. Name the block that starts drawing with the pen
   _____HINT *Puts the pen down on the screen*

5. Name the block that stops drawing with the pen
   _____HINT *Takes the pen up from the screen*

Pink

Look at the code inside the pink sprite

6. Why are there two move blocks (move 120 steps) and (move 30 steps)?

Now mark the investigate questions using the answer sheet

Supporting INVESTIGATE

Whole class advice

Work in pairs, one device between the pair. Take it in turns every question to swap who runs code. You must work at the same pace as your partner and not move on to the next question until you have both written your answer down. If you disagree write a different answer. You must mark your work before moving on to the next section.

Notes on the activity

Investigating the code encourages pupils to think deeply about how it works. Check that every pupil is filling in and marking the questions individually but at the pace of the slowest in the pair. Sometimes a pair decides not to mark to speed up their efforts. Marking gives valuable information, so I recommend sending them back to mark their work. A class instruction to come and talk to you if they have over half of the questions wrong or they do not understand the answer after they have marked it helps to check progress is being made correctly. There is real value in collecting these scores to build up a summative picture of pupil progress.

Investigate the Code

Run the programs lots of times to help you answer the questions but do not change anything. Run each shape a few times using the a, b, c, d and e keys.

Look at the code inside the **blue** sprite

1. How many times will **move 40 steps** be run?
   4 (1 mark)
2. How many times will **wait 1 seconds** be run?
   8 (1 mark) (2, 4 or 8)

Blue

Q1 Ask how many times it will go through the loop?

Q2 Ask if there was only one wait block how many times would it be run? So as there are two how many times now?

Look at the code inside the purple sprite

3. How many times will **turn left 60 degrees** be run? 6 (1 mark)
4. Name the block that starts drawing with the pen
   _____HINT *Puts the pen down on the screen*
5. Name the block that stops drawing with the pen
   _____Hint *Takes the pen up from the screen*

Purple

Q3 Ask how many times it will go through the loop?

Q4 & 5 Ask pupil if they have to put the pen down on the page to write or pull the pen up to stop writing.

Look at the code inside the pink sprite

6. Why are there two move blocks (move 120 steps) and (move 30 steps)?

Now mark the investigate questions using the answer sheet

Pink

Q6 Ask them to draw the shape following the instructions in the loop. Drawing 30mm and 120mm or 3cm and 12cm.

Send advice

Support pairs of pupils who are poor readers by reading questions, reading code samples and covering up questions until they get to them.

Exploring 2D Shapes
FLOW

Don't load
Scratch

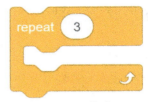

Count-Controlled Loop

Draw the flow of control on these code sections as a line.

Add a dot for every action.

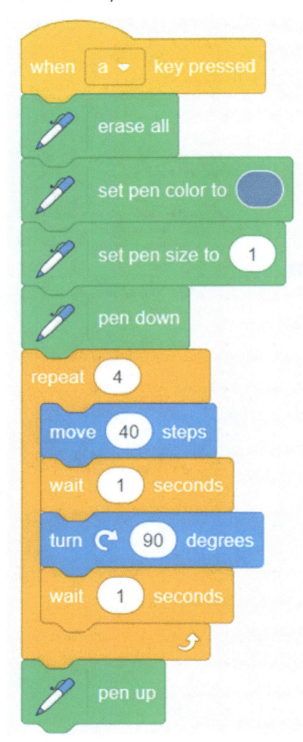

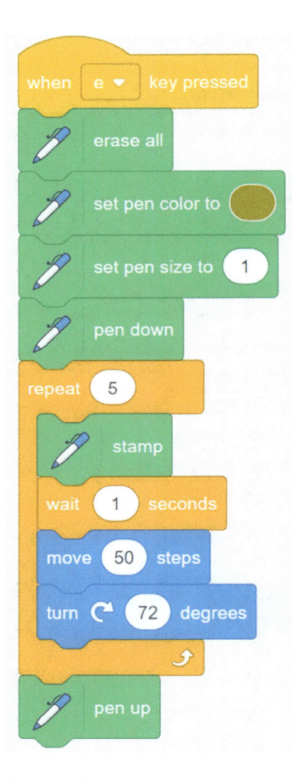

Now mark the drawing the flow of control questions using the answer sheet

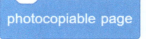

Supporting FLOW

Whole class instructions

Look at this code carefully. Now draw the flow of control on top of the code as a line and each action as a dot. Be sure to show where the count-controlled loop is.

Notes on the activity

This activity builds on the concept introduction and could be completed directly after it instead of in the order provided here. It could also be used to work with SEN pupils only.

Draw the flow of control on these code sections as a line.

Add a dot for every action.

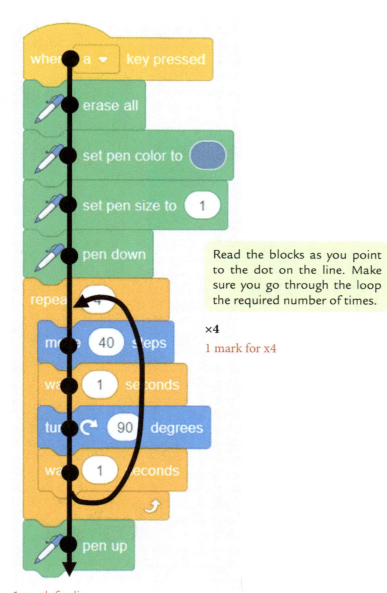

Read the blocks as you point to the dot on the line. Make sure you go through the loop the required number of times.

×4

1 mark for x4

1 mark for line
1 mark for dots in the right place

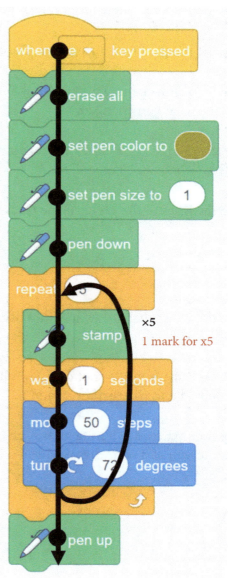

×5

1 mark for x5

1 mark for line
1 mark for dots in the right place

Exploring 2D Shapes
CHANGE

Work with a partner

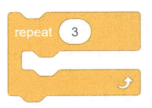

Count-Controlled Loop

Change Make changes to one of the numbers in the code

1. Make the **blue** square **larger**. Describe what you changed.

2. Make the **pink** rectangle **longer**. Describe what you changed.

3. Make the **purple** hexagon **smaller**. Describe what you changed.

4. Make the **yellow** pentagon only draw **four** of its five sides. Describe what you changed.

5. **Slow** the **purple** hexagon down so that it draws the shape **slower**. Describe what you changed.

6. Make the **lines** of the **green** shape **thicker**. Describe what you changed.

Change or Add

You might need to change something that is not a number or add code

7. Make the blue square draw the lines using a **different colour**. Describe what you changed.

8. Make each shape sprite (not orange) **tell the user what its name is after** it has drawn itself. What did you add and where did you add it?

9. Make the square **play a note after** each line is drawn. What did you add and where did you add it?

Q9 HINT   Music
Play instruments and drums.

Mark your work using the answer sheet

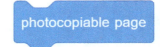

photocopiable page

SUPPORTING CHANGE

Whole class advice

Work in pairs, one device between the pair. Take it in turns every question to swap who runs code. You must work at the same pace as your partner and not move on to the next question until you have both written your answer down. If you disagree write a different answer. You must mark your work before moving on to the next section.

If pupils are struggling on a specific question draw their attention to the bold text as they are clues.

Notes on the activity

This activity builds on the concept introduction and could be completed directly after it instead of in the order provided here. It could also be used to work with SEN pupils only.

Whole class advice

Remind pupils that for the first seven questions they only need to change a number and that it is fine to change a number and find that it did not work and so change it back.

Change Make changes to one of the numbers in the code

1. Make the **blue** square **larger**. Describe what you changed.

   Change move 50 steps to a higher number (1 mark)

2. Make the **pink** rectangle **longer**. Describe what you changed.

   Change move 120 steps to a higher number (1 mark)

3. Make the **purple** hexagon **smaller**. Describe what you changed.

   Change move 45 steps to a lower number (1 mark)

4. Make the **yellow** pentagon only draw **four** of its five sides. Describe what you changed.

   Change repeat 5 to repeat 4 (1 mark)

5. **Slow** the **purple** hexagon down so that it draws the shape **slower**. Describe what you changed.

   Change one of both of the wait blocks to any number larger than 0.5 seconds (1 mark)

6. Make the **lines** of the **green** shape **thicker**. Describe what you changed.

   Change set pen size to any number higher than 1 (1 mark)

Change or Add

You might need to change something that is not a number or add code

7. Make the blue square draw the lines using a **different colour**. Describe what you changed.

   Change set pen color [US spelling] (UK spelling colour) to any other colour (1 mark)

8. Make each shape sprite (not orange) **tell the user what its name is after** it has drawn itself. What did you add and where did you add it?

   Add a say or think block or record a sound block and add them at the end of each script. (1 mark)

9. Make the square **play a note after** each line is drawn. What did you add and where did you add it?

   Add a play note block inside the loop after the move block (1 mark)

Mark your work using the answer sheet

Q1 What code draws the side of the shape? Answer Move and the pen down.

Q2 What code draws the longest side of the shape?

Q3 What code draws the side of the shape?

Q4 What code controls how many sides are drawn? Answer the loop.

Q5 Look for time-related code.

Q6 What controls the line size?

Q7 You may wish to point out the US spelling of colour.

Q9 Pupils will often need a reminder of where the music blocks can be found despite fact there is a hint on the page.

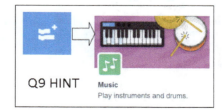

Q9 HINT Music
Play instruments and drums.

Whole class advice

Remind pupils that every time they try something that does not work they are learning more and helping to build their understanding of how the code works.

**Exploring 2D Shapes
CREATE**

Work on
your own

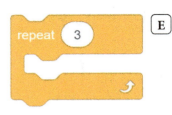

Count-Controlled Loop

Challenge 1 Turn the plan below into code using the blocks inside the Orange sprite

Idea Level	Planning Level

Program a sprite to draw a triangle	**Algorithm**
	Start with f key
	Wipe out all previous lines
	Make line colour orange
	Pen thickness 3
	Pen down to start drawing
	Loop 3 times
	    Move 50
	    Turn right 120 degrees
	    Stamp
	    Pause 1 second
	Pen up to stop drawing

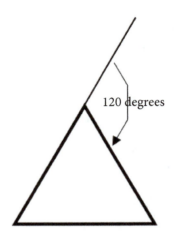

120 degrees

Challenge 2 Copy a sprite and adapt the code to draw an octagon (8 sided shape), **nonagon** (9 sided shape) **or heptagon** (7 sided shape) **using the information below.**

Name of the shape	Heptagon (7 sides)	Octagon (8 sides)	Nonagon (9 sides)
Part of outer angle	51.5 Degrees	45 Degrees	40 Degrees

Challenge 3 Build the code below. Experiment with it to create fun patterns

Change the code to

1. Make the patterns repeat for a full circle.
2. Make it change colour every time it draws a line. *HINT Change pen colour by number.*
3. Make repeated patterns with less points.
4. Make repeated patterns with more points.

Teacher and pupil Assessment

Circle how much work you have completed. Your teacher will check it.

	Completed no challenges	Completed challenge 1 only	Completed challenge 1 and 2	Completed 1 and 2 and three or more of challenge 3
Count controlled Loops	0 marks	1 mark	2 marks	3 marks

photocopiable page

Supporting CREATE

Whole class advice

Work on your own, one device each. You can discuss the work with your former partner but you are responsible for creating your own projects. Save your work regularly. Read the instructions carefully. Assess your own work by circling where you think you are in the assessment grid at the bottom of the page.

Notes on the activity

The make part of a project is really important and teachers should always make sure that pupils have time to make their own project, even if that means reducing the time spent on other stages for pupils who work slowly. It helps if pupils work on their own for this while supporting their partner.

Challenge 1 Turn the plan below into code using the blocks inside the orange sprite

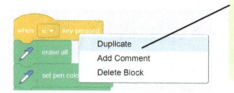

It can be helpful to show all pupils how they can duplicate code by finding the top block on a script they want to duplicate and right clicking and selecting duplicate.

Idea Level	Planning Level

Program a sprite to draw a triangle	**Algorithm**
	Start with f key
	Wipe out all previous lines
	Make line colour orange
	Pen thickness 3
	Pen down to start drawing
	Loop 3 times
	    Move 50
	    Turn right 120 degrees
	    Stamp
	    Pause 1 second
	Pen up to stop drawing

Challenge 1 If pupils are struggling, remind them that the algorithm plan will not be written in Scratch code so should be different. Are there keywords in a line? Can they find similar words in the code?

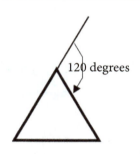

120 degrees

Challenge 1 To avoid misunderstanding it can be helpful to mark out a triangle and walk over it. Making the point that the angle turned is part of the outer angle rather than the inner angle.

Challenge 2 Copy a sprite and adapt the code to draw an octagon (eight-sided shape), **nonagon** (nine-sided shape) **and heptagon** (seven-sided shape) **using the information below**.

Name of the shape	Heptagon (seven sides)	Octagon (eight sides)	Nonagon (nine sides)
Part of outer angle	51.5 Degrees	45 Degrees	40 Degrees

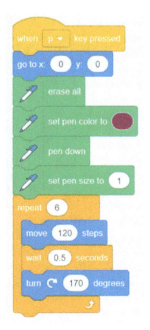

Challenge 3 Build the code below. Experiment with it to create fun patterns

You could adapt it to

1. Make the patterns repeat for a full circle.
2. Make it change colour every time it draws a line. *HINT Change pen colour by number.*
3. Make repeated patterns with less points.
4. Make repeated patterns with more points.

Challenge 2 When you are assessing these check to see if shapes finish exactly where they started. If pupils have changed the angle but not the number of loops it indicates that understanding is partial.

Challenge 2 It can help to remind pupils how they can right click and duplicate the square. Then point out the two changes needed to make it a heptagon. Ask how they will change the sides to 7? How will they change the degrees to 51.5.

See marksheet for more info

Assessment: Remind pupils to self-assess and later Check if pupils' selfassessment is correct.

	Completed no challenges	Completed challenge 1 only	Completed challenge 1 and 2	Completed 1 and 2 and three or more of challenge 3
Count controlled Loops	0 marks	1 mark	2 marks	3 marks

Exploring 2D Shapes
Parsons Marksheet

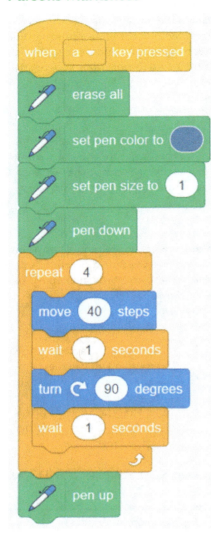

1 mark

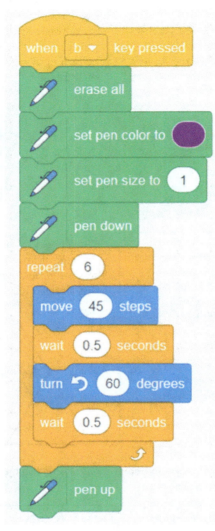

1 mark

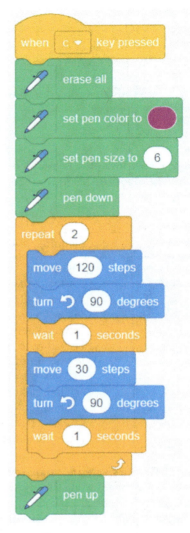

1 mark

photocopiable page

Exploring 2D Shapes
Predict Marksheet

F

1. **Read the code carefully and complete the table**

	Blue Shape	Purple Shape	Pink Shape
Number of repeats	4 (1 mark)	6	2 (1 mark)
Move steps number	40 (1 mark)	45 (1 mark)	120 and 30
Turn in degrees	90	60 (1 mark)	90 (1 mark)

2. **Match the code with what it does**

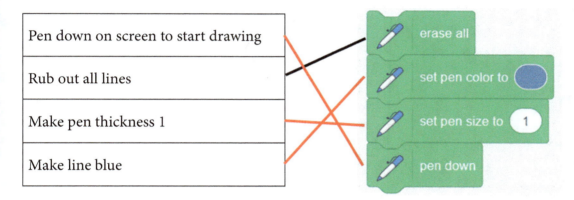

Pen down on screen to start drawing
Rub out all lines
Make pen thickness 1
Make line blue

erase all

set pen color to

set pen size to 1

pen down

3. **Predict what shape it will draw by drawing a line from sprite to shape**

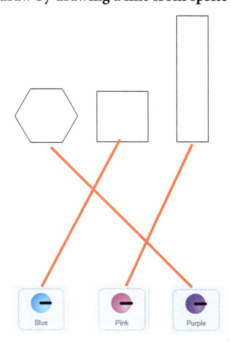

Exploring 2D Shapes
Investigate Marksheet

G

Look at the code inside the blue sprite

Blue

1. How many times will **move 40 steps** be run?
    4 (1 mark)
2. How many times will wait 1 seconds be run?
    8 (1 mark)(2, 4 or 8)

Look at the code inside the purple sprite

Purple

3. How many times will **turn left 60 degrees** be run?
    6 (1 mark)
4. Name the block that starts drawing with the pen
    pen down (1 mark) *HINT Puts the pen down on the screen*
5. Name the block that stops drawing with the pen
    pen up (1 mark) *Hint Takes the pen up from the screen*

Look at the code inside the pink sprite

Pink

6. Why are there two move blocks (move 120 steps) and (move 30 steps)?
    Any answer that indicates that the shape has a pair of long side and
    pair of short sides or mentions a rectangle by name (2 marks)

Exploring 2D Shapes
Flow Marksheet

Draw the flow of control on these code sections.
Add a dot for every action.

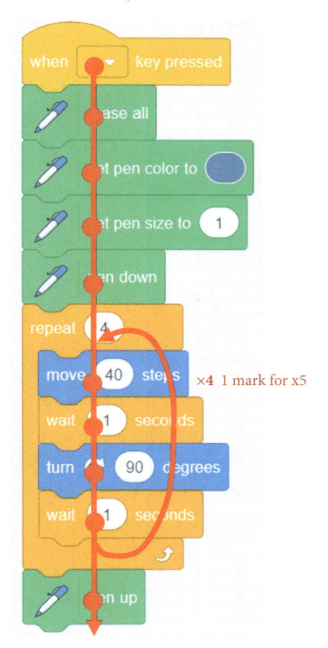

×4 1 mark for x5

1 mark for line
1 mark for dots in the right place

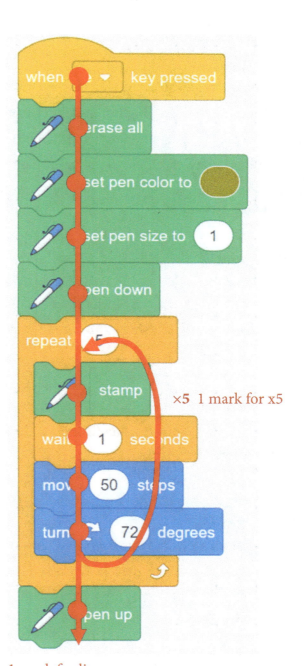

×5 1 mark for x5

1 mark for line
1 mark for dots in the right place

Exploring 2D Shapes
Change Marksheet

I

Change Make changes to one of the numbers in the code

1. Make the **blue** square **larger**. Describe what you changed.

   Change move 50 steps to a higher number (1 mark)

2. Make the **pink** rectangle **longer**. Describe what you changed.

   Change move 120 steps to a higher number (1 mark)

3. Make the **purple** hexagon **smaller**. Describe what you changed.

   Change move 45 steps to a lower number (1 mark)

4. Make the pentagon only draw four of its five sides.
   Describe what you changed.

   Change repeat 5 to repeat 4 (1 mark)

5. **Slow** the **purple** hexagon down so that it draws the shape **slower**.
   Describe what you changed.

   Change one of both of the wait blocks to any number larger than 0.5 seconds (1 mark)

6. Make the **lines** of the **green** shape **thicker**. Describe what you changed.

   Change set pen size to any number higher than 1 (1 mark)

Change or Add

You might need to change something that is not a number or add code

7. Make the blue square draw the lines using a **different colour**.
   Describe what you changed.

   Change set pen color [US spelling] (UK spelling: colour) to any other colour (1 mark)

8. Make each shape sprite **tell the user what its name is after** it has drawn itself. What did you add and where did you add it?

   Add a say or think block or record a sound block and add them at the end of each script. (1 mark)

9. Make the square **play a note after** each line is drawn.
   What did you add and where did you add it?

   Add a play note block inside the loop after the move block (1 mark)

Exploring 2D Shapes
Create Marksheet

J

Challenge 1 Turn the plan below into code using the blocks inside the orange sprite

Idea Level	Planning Level
Program a sprite to draw a triangle	**Algorithm** Start with f key Wipe out all previous lines Make line colour orange Pen thickness 3 Pen down to start drawing Loop 3 times Move 50 Turn right 120 degrees Stamp Pause 1 second Pen up to stop drawing

(1 mark) if all your initialisation code that makes the shape, run the same way each is in this order

(1 mark) if all your code inside the loop is in this order

(1 mark) if all your pen up is outside the loop NOT inside it

Challenge 2 Copy a sprite and adapt the code to draw an octagon (eight-sided shape), **nonagon** (nine-sided shape) **and Heptagon** (seven-sided shape) **using the information below.**

Name of the shape	Heptagon (seven sides)	Octagon (eight sides)	Nonagon (nine sides)
Part of outer angle	51.5 Degrees	45 Degrees	40 Degrees

(1 mark) for every correct repeat

(1 mark) for every correct angle

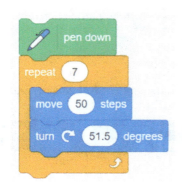
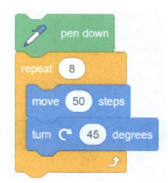
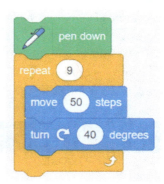

Moves can be different
Turns could be right or left
There could be other code

Challenge 3 Build the code below. Experiment with it to create fun patterns

You could adapt it to

- Make the patterns repeat for a full circle
- Make it change colour every time it draws a line *HINT Change pen colour by number*
- Make repeated patterns with fewer points
- Make repeated patterns with more points

Your teacher will look at your Challenge 3 patterns and mark them.

Overview

Pupils explore how Scratch can move characters using count-controlled loops before creating their own moving character who interacts with other characters.

To do before the session

1. Look at the grid below and decide which optional and SEN activities you are going to include and exclude.
2. Print pupil worksheets for each activity chosen and staple into a booklet, one for each pupil.
3. Print marksheets for activities chosen to be placed where pupils can access them.
4. Download the code needed and place in a templates folder on your school network or add to a Scratch Studio or link on your learning platform.
5. Download the slides that go with the concept introduction.
6. Study the notes that go with the slides.
7. Examine the teacher help notes that are provided alongside every activity.

To do at the start of the session

If you have not introduced count-controlled loops with this class before, do this first as a whole class activity.

To do after the concept has been introduced

Each activity has whole class notes to help you explain what is needed if it is the first time pupils have carried out this type of activity. There are also core instructions underneath in case you are sticking to the core activities only.

How this module fits into a programming progression

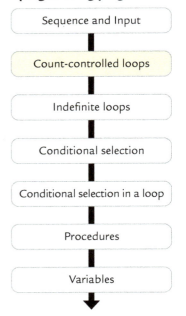

Sequence and Input

Count-controlled loops

Indefinite loops

Conditional selection

Conditional selection in a loop

Procedures

Variables

Vocabulary

Count-controlled loop, loop, repeat, do x times. Sprite, costume, backdrop, position, motion, degrees, direction, keyboard

NOTE This module does not have a PARSONS element as there is a lot of code to build.

Flow of control is built into PREDICT and there is a support sheet at the end of the module.

This module is a really good one to do if pupils have already encountered count control looks in one of the earlier projects.

Resource Name	Core Optional SEN	Teacher	Pupil Grouping	How Assessed	SCRATCH ACCESS
CONCEPT Count-controlled loop (page)	CORE	Leads Session	Solo whole class activity	Formative	NO
PREDICT	OPTIONAL ALL	Support Poor Readers	Paired	Pupil Marked Marksheet Provided	NO
INVESTIGATE	CORE	Support Poor Readers	Paired	Pupil Marked Marksheet Provided	YES Come back doggy!
CHANGE	CORE	Support Poor Readers	Paired	Pupil Marked Marksheet Provided	YES Come back doggy!
PLAN	CORE	Leads Session OR Supports pupils	Solo OR Whole class activity		NO
CREATE	CORE	Assesses pupil work and checks pupil self-assessment	Solo	Pupil Assessed & Teacher Assessed	YES Come back doggy!

(Yellow is core module, pink and white are optional.)

Core activities general instructions

1. Group pupils in roughly same ability pairs. For investigate and change worksheets, pupils will work in pairs, for create they will work separately.

2. Give out the pupil booklets and explain that pupils need to follow the instructions on the sheets to explore how count-controlled loops work.

3. Explain that each pupil will record separately while working alongside their partner and keeping to the same pace as their partner

4. Demonstrate where they can find the template code and explain that pupils will share one device for investigate and change.

5. Explain that during each question only one person should touch the shared device and they should swap who that person is when there is a new questions.

6. Encourage them to discuss their answers with their partner. If they disagree with their partner, they can record a different answer in their own booklet.

7. Show pupils where it says they should mark their work on the sheet and where the answer sheets are in the classroom.

8. Remind pupils to return marksheets after marking, because there are not enough for every pair to have their own.

Key Programming Knowledge
A loop is any set of instructions that are repeated
An algorithm is any set of instructions to carry out a task that can be understood by another human

A count-controlled loop
Can replace a sequence where there is a pattern.
Is controlled by the number
Ends after the number of repeats are complete
Is called a repeat loop in Scratch programming
Has a flow of control (order that commands are run in)
Can be used in an algorithm or in programming

Resources
Come Back Doggy!   https://scratch.mit.edu/projects/508314407/

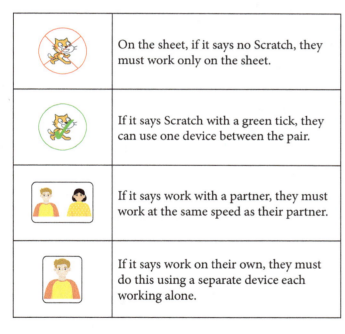

(no Scratch icon)	On the sheet, if it says no Scratch, they must work only on the sheet.
(Scratch with green tick icon)	If it says Scratch with a green tick, they can use one device between the pair.
(two people icon)	If it says work with a partner, they must work at the same speed as their partner.
(one person icon)	If it says work on their own, they must do this using a separate device each working alone.

The First Software Loop
The scholarly consensus is that the first instance of a software loop was the loop **Ada Lovelace** used to calculate Bernoulli numbers using **Charles Babbage's** Analytical Engine mechanical computer

Scottish Curriculum for Excellence Technologies
I understand the instructions of a visual programming language and can predict the outcome of a program written using the language. TCH 1-14a

I can explain core programming language concepts in appropriate technical language TCH 2-14a

I can demonstrate a range of basic problem solving skills by building simple programs to carry out a given task, using an appropriate language. TCH 1-15a

I can create, develop and evaluate computing solutions in response to a design challenge. TCH 2-15a

English Computing National Curriculum Programs of Study

Pupils should be taught to:

- **design, write and debug programs that accomplish specific goals**, including controlling or simulating physical systems; solve problems by decomposing them into smaller parts

- **use sequence**, selection and **repetition in programs**; work with variables **and various forms of input and output**

- **use logical reasoning to explain how some simple algorithms work and to detect and correct** errors in algorithms and programs

Welsh National Curriculum Relevant Strands
Progression Step 3.

- I can identify repeating patterns and use loops to make my algorithms more concise.

- I can explain and debug algorithms.

Come Back Doggy!

Predict

Work with a partner

Don't load Scratch

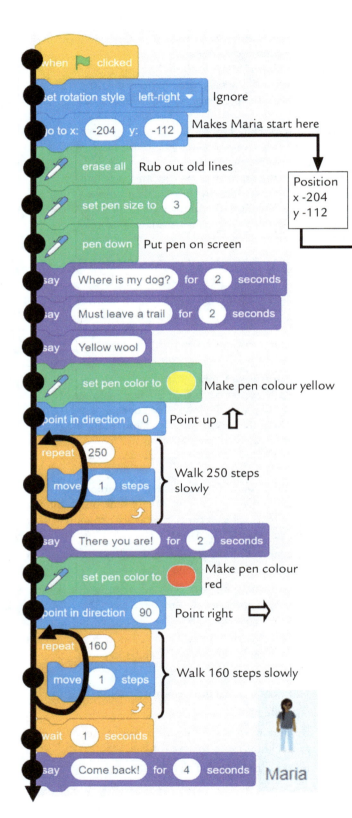

when ⚑ clicked

set rotation style [left-right ▾] — Ignore

go to x: (-204) y: (-112) — Makes Maria start here

🖊 erase all — Rub out old lines

🖊 set pen size to (3)

🖊 pen down — Put pen on screen

say [Where is my dog?] for (2) seconds

say [Must leave a trail] for (2) seconds

say [Yellow wool]

🖊 set pen color to ⬤ — Make pen colour yellow

point in direction (0) — Point up ⬆

repeat (250)
 move (1) steps
— Walk 250 steps slowly

say [There you are!] for (2) seconds

🖊 set pen color to ⬤ — Make pen colour red

point in direction (90) — Point right ➡

repeat (160)
 move (1) steps
— Walk 160 steps slowly

wait (1) seconds

say [Come back!] for (4) seconds — Maria

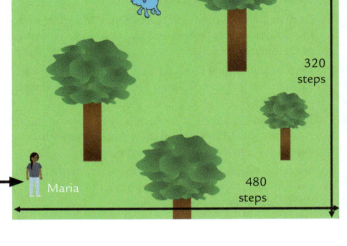

Position
x -204
y -112

320 steps

480 steps

Maria

Read the code from top to bottom. Take it in turns to tell your partner what you think it does. There are some clues to help you.

Work out where Maria is programmed to go on the map above.

HINT Look at the point in direction blocks and the repeat loops.

1. Draw a line where you think she will go first.

2. Draw a line where you think she will go second.

3. Next to both lines write what colours you think they will be. *HINT Do not be put off by the American spelling of colour (color).*

4. Next to both lines write how many steps you think they will be. *HINT Repeat loop.*

Supporting Predict

Whole class advice

Make sure you work with your partner on this sheet. Take it in turns to read a section and tell your partner what you think it does. Then answer the questions using your understanding of the code.

Notes on the activity

This optional activity helps pupils to think about the bigger purpose of the program before they start looking at parts of it in later sections.

Send support

It can really help pupils to see a move 1 step block inside a repeat 100 loop separate from all other code.

You might also want to pretend you are in a loop and act out moving one step repeatedly.

Send support

Support pairs of pupils who are poor readers by reading questions, reading code samples and covering up questions until they get to them.

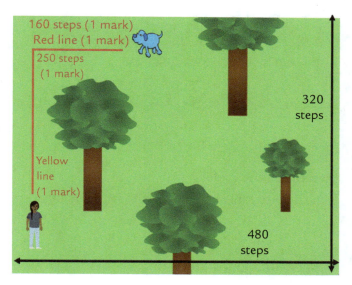

Read the code from top to bottom. Take it in turns to tell your partner what you think it does. There are some clues to help you.

Often pupils do not want to take the trouble to read the code block by block. Work with them asking them what they think each code will do. When you get to the move blocks inside the repeat blocks act out moving one step and repeating it.

Try and work out where Maria is programmed to go on the map above.

HINT Look at the point in direction blocks and the repeat loops.

Q1 Explain the go to x and y block places Maria where we find her on the map shown. That is her starting point. What will the code make her travel?

Q3 Say if only there was a block that showed you what colour the line is now and walk away.

Q4 Say you are inside a loop 5 times move 1 step algorithm. How many steps will you take?

Send support

If you have a child who is put of by lots of test there is a plan version of the flow of control at the end of the chapter.

1. Draw a line where you think she will go first?

   (1 mark) for a line up from Maria as shown

2. Draw a line where you think she will go second?

   (1 mark) for a line across the top joining to first line as show above

3. Next to both lines write what colours you think they will be? *HINT Do not be put off by the American spelling of colour (color).*

   Yellow and then red marked on lines in correct places (2 marks)

4. Next to both lines write how many steps you think they will be?

   First line 250 steps second line 160 steps (2 possible marks)

Come Back Doggy!
INVESTIGATE

Work with a partner

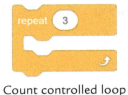

Count controlled loop

Start Scratch and load the
Come Back Doggy! program

Play Come Back Doggy! a few times. The green flag starting block will start the program.

Mark your reading code and predicting what it will do questions from the last sheet

Investigate the code
Run the programs lots of times to help you answer the questions but don't change the code

Look at the code inside Maria
Maria sprite questions

Maria

1. Which block starts the code?

2. What block makes Maria go back to the start? (Initialization) *HINT go to*

3. Which block rubs out any old lines before Maria searches for her dog? (Initialization)

4. In the first repeat loop (count-controlled loop), how many times will move 1 step be run?

5. Which loop draws the shortest line?

6. Which block changes Maria's direction?

Look at the code inside the dog
Dog sprite questions

7. Which line of code makes the dog wait until Maria arrives?

8. Which blocks get repeated 21 times?

9. What direction (up, down, right or left) does point in direction 180 make the dog go?

Now mark the investigate questions using the answer sheet

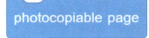

Come Back Doggy!
Supporting INVESTIGATE

Play Come Back Doggy! a few times. The green flag starting block will start the program.

Mark your reading code and predicting what it will do questions from the last sheet

Investigate the code
Run the programs lots of times to help you answer the questions but don't change the code.

Maria

Look at the code inside Maria
Maria sprite questions

1. Which block starts the code?

   Green flag (1 mark)

2. What block makes Maria go back to the start? (Initialization) HINT go to

   go to x and y (1 mark)

3. Which block rubs out any old lines before Maria searches for her dog? (Initialization)

   Erase all (1 mark)

4. In the first repeat loop (count-controlled loop), how many times will move 1 step be run?

   250 (1 mark)

5. Which loop draws the shortest line?

   Repeat 160 or the second repeat loop (1 mark)

6. Which block changes Maria's direction?

   Point in direction (1 mark)

Look at the code inside the Dog

Dog Sprite Questions

7. Which line of code makes the dog wait until Maria arrives?

   Wait until touching Maria (1 mark)

8. Which blocks get repeated 21 times?

   Next costume (1 mark) wait 0.4 seconds (1 mark)

9. What direction (up, down, right or left) does point in direction 180 make the dog go?

   Down (1 mark)

Now mark the investigate questions using the answer sheet

Notes on the activity
Investigating the code encourages pupils to think deeply about how it works. Check that every pupil is filling in and marking the questions individually but at the pace of the slowest in the pair. Sometimes a pair decides not to mark to speed up their efforts. Marking gives valuable information, so I recommend sending them back to mark their work. A class instruction to come and talk to you if they have over half of the questions wrong or they do not understand the answer after they have marked it helps to check progress is being made correctly. There is real value in collecting these scores to build up a summative picture of pupil progress.

Q2 Code initialization – the idea that we need to write code to make sure the program resets itself before running again is a hard concept, so it is important to drip feed this in every project. Why not add it to your spellings or word wall.

Q2 Pupils don't need to understand x and y at this moment it is enough to know that these numbers make the code go to a place on the screen. Dragging a sprite to the place you want it to start from and then dragging an x and y block will give it the correct coordinate reference points.

Q4 You can sometimes help by simplifying.

Say you are inside a loop 5 times move 1 step algorithm. How many steps will you take?

Q5 Repeat 10 with move 1 inside would move 10 steps. Repeat 50 with move 1 would move 50 steps.

Q6 Keyword direction.

Q7 Wait until touching is a condition which we will explore in much more depth next year. In Year 3 and 4, we are sticking to wait until <insert condition> blocks wait until a key is pressed or wait until a colour is touched are other common ones. These are simple enough to understand in a concrete way.

Q9 Click on the direction block to show a direction dial.

Come Back Doggy!
CHANGE

Work with a partner

Count controlled loop

Start Scratch and load the
Come Back Doggy! program

Look at the code inside the Maria sprite
Make small changes to the code

Maria

1. Can you make Maria stop just before she touches the dog?
   What did you change? *HINT Repeat loop*

2. Can you make Maria bump into the tree after she catches up with the dog?
   What did you change? *HINT Repeat loop*

Look at the code inside the Dog sprite
Make small changes to the code

3. Can you make the dog say something after the girl bumps into him?
   HINT Wait until touching... What code did you add? Where did you add it?

4. Can you make the dog's legs look like they are walking slower?
   What did you change?

Now mark the changing code questions using the answer sheet

Come Back Doggy!
CHANGE

Whole class advice

Work in pairs, one device between the pair. Take it in turns every question to swap who runs code. You must work at the same pace as your partner and not move on to the next question until you have both written your answer down. If you disagree, write a different answer. You must mark your work before moving on to the next section.

Send advice

Support pairs of pupils who are poor readers by reading questions, reading code samples and covering up questions until they get to them.

Maria

Look at the code inside the Maria sprite
Make small changes to the code

1. Can you make Maria stop just before she touches the dog? What did you change? *HINT Repeat loop*

    Change repeat 160 to a number less than 130 (1 mark)

2. Can you make Maria bump into the tree after she catches up with the dog?
    What did you change? *HINT Repeat loop*

    Change repeat 160 to a number more than 220 (1 mark)

Look at the code inside the dog sprite
Make small changes to the code

3. Can you make the dog say something after the girl bumps into him?
    HINT Wait until touching…

    What code did you add? Add a say or sound block (1 mark)
    Where did you add it? Add it after the wait until touching Maria in either script (1 mark)

4. Can you make the dogs legs look like they are walking slower? What did you change?

    Change the wait inside the repeat 21 loop to a higher number, such as 1 second (1 mark)

Now mark the changing code questions using the answer sheet

Notes on the activity

Changing or modifying code is a core part of this module so I suggest you do not leave it out. It is an important step towards creation of their own code as parts they have modified they will feel more ownership of. Recording marks will help with assessment.

Q1 Model this by simplifying it. Move a couple of metres away from the pair. Say I am in a repeat 3 count-controlled loop. Then walk and say move one step for each loop. Move back to the start and ask them how they can get you to stop before you reach them.

Q1 It is also possible to solve this by changing move 1 step to a number less than 1, such as move 0.7 steps.

Q2 The tree in question is the one to the right of her.

Q2 It is also possible to solve this by changing move 1 step to a number more than 1, such as move 2 steps.

Q3 If a pupil places a say block inside a loop, ask them why they want this to be repeated many times. Whilst it does answer the question it is not the best place to place a say block. If other code is present in the loop, it will slow the loop down, which may affect the other code.

Q4 Ask pupils to underline key words in the question. Make sure they identify slower.

Say slower is a time word. Are their any time words in the code that makes the dogs legs look like they are moving?

This is normally enough of a hint so best to walk away to allow them to process it.

Come Back Doggy!
PLAN

Have a look at the plan for a similar program to Come Back Doggy!, where a bird flew around clouds and bumped into stars. Can you spot the planning algorithms for point in directions and repeat loops?

photocopiable page

Count-controlled loop

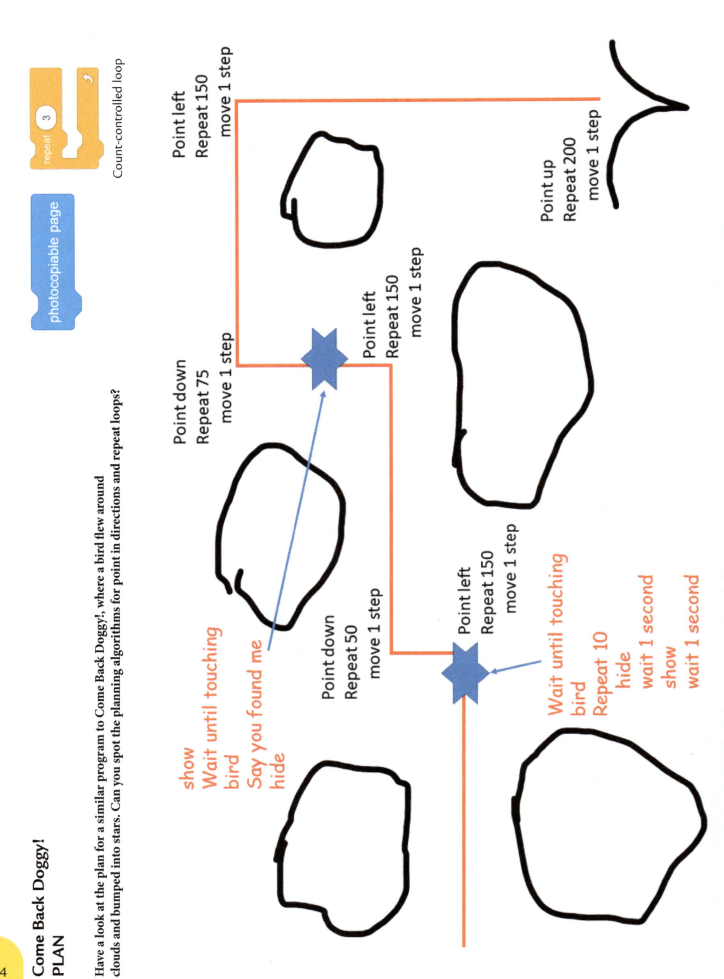

Point left
Repeat 150
move 1 step

Point up
Repeat 200
move 1 step

Point down
Repeat 75
move 1 step

Point left
Repeat 150
move 1 step

Point down
Repeat 50
move 1 step

Point left
Repeat 150
move 1 step

show
Wait until touching
bird
Say you found me
hide

Wait until touching
bird
Repeat 10
hide
wait 1 second
show
wait 1 second

Come Back Doggy!
PLAN

Have a look at the plan for a similar program to Come Back Doggy!, where a bird flew around clouds and bumped into stars. Can you spot the planning algorithms for point in directions and repeat loops?

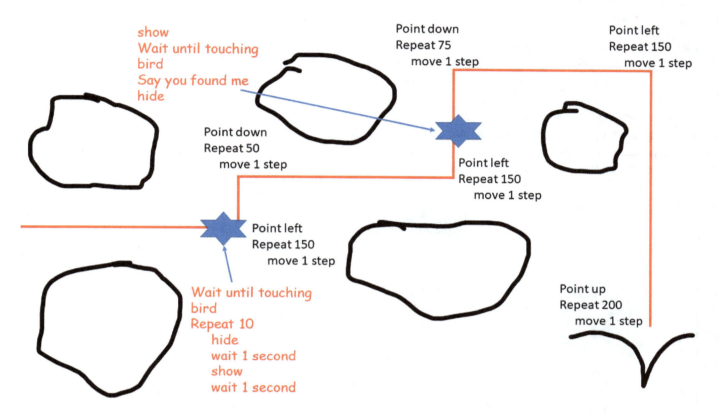

show
Wait until touching bird
Say you found me
hide

Point down
Repeat 75
   move 1 step

Point left
Repeat 150
   move 1 step

Point down
Repeat 50
   move 1 step

Point left
Repeat 150
   move 1 step

Point left
Repeat 150
   move 1 step

Wait until touching bird
Repeat 10
   hide
   wait 1 second
   show
   wait 1 second

Point up
Repeat 200
   move 1 step

Whole class advice

If you choose to get the whole class to make a new project (top project on next sheet), then you might want to go through the process above with your class planning their own projects after you model a step. This will ensure a much higher standard or planning which will improve creation.

Notes on the activity

Because there is nothing they need to mark or hand in, pupils often skip over this example planning page. However planning really does improve the quality of pupils' programming output. To stop this you could

Talk through the sheet with the whole class, hence raising its status

Draw your own version step by step in this order

1. Decide on a theme
2. Choose a sprite
3. Place obstacles
4. Draw a path
5. Add directions
6. Add loops

Come Back Doggy! CREATE

Plan and Create New OR Plan and Create Inside Come Back Doggy!

Count controlled loop

Plan and create new

Design and make your own moving scene using a move block inside a repeat block. Use a sheet of plain A4 paper turned landscape view to plan on. Use the plan on the last page to help you, draw obstacles, draw sprite start, draw pathway, add directions, write move inside loop algorithms.

Plan and create inside come back doggy!

1. Design and program your own route through the trees for Maria to take. Keep the code and modify it. Create a plan on the picture below using the plan on the last page to help you.

2. Add another character to the woods that the Maria meets. Program the character to do or say something when Maria touches them.

3. Program a tree to say or do something when the Maria touches it.

4. Draw a spider sprite that drops out of a tree using the pen command as its web. Drag the sprite to its start position and drag out a go to x and y block so the spider always starts in the same position (initialization).

Teacher & Pupil Assessment	Circle the stage that you think you have reached in each row, your teacher will check it.		
	Not used a count control loop	Used a count control loop to move a character	Used a count controlled loop to move a character and has used a count controlled loop independently for some other purpose
Count-controlled Loops	0 Marks	1 mark	2 marks

		Not used previous programming concepts for real purpose	Used previous programming concepts for real purpose
Used previous programming concept such as sequence and inputs		0 Marks	1 mark

		No theme in planning or code	Has a simple theme in planning or code	Has an interesting or amusing theme in planning or code
Has a project theme in planning or code		0 Marks	1 mark	2 marks

SUPPORTING CREATE

Plan and Create New OR Plan and Create Inside Come Back Doggy!

Whole class advice

Work on your own, one device each. You can discuss the work with your former partner but you are responsible for creating your own projects. Save your work regularly. Read the instructions carefully. Assess your own work by circling where you think you are in the assessment grid at the bottom of the page.

Plan and create new

Design and make your own moving scene using a move block inside a repeat block. Use a sheet of plain A4 paper turned landscape view to plan on. Use the plan on the last page to help you, draw obstacles, draw sprite start, draw pathway, add directions, write move inside loop algorithms.

Plan and make inside come back doggy!

1. Design and program your own route through the trees for Maria to take. Keep the code and modify it. Create a plan on the picture below using the plan on the last page to help you.

2. Add another character to the woods that Maria meets. Program the character to do or say something when Maria touches them.

3. Program a tree to say or do something when Maria touches it.

4. Draw a spider sprite that drops out of a tree using the pen command as its web. Drag the sprite to its start position and drag out a go to x and y block so the spider always starts in the same position (initialization).

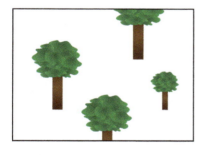

Notes on the activity

The make part of a project is really important and teachers should always make sure that pupils have time to make their own project, even if that means reducing the time spent on other stages for pupils who work slowly. It helps if pupils work on their own for this whilst supporting their partner.

INSIDE Come Back Doggy. This project has the benefit of keeping all the code that pupils have investigated and modified in easy reach, which makes it an easier option for most pupils.

Seeing themselves in the sprite

Many pupils may wish to change the main sprite to make it represent them and their community. Scratch 3 has some new sprites that make this much easier. Look for Characters 1 and 2 who have multiple costumes representing many diverse backgrounds.

Characters 1   Characters 2

Instructing pupils to plan a bit and then make it before repeating the process can help to keep them more motivated.

Reminding pupils of the planning criteria will help to keep pupils focussed on quality outcomes that demonstrate the concept you are working on (count-controlled loops).

There are some notes on how you might improve this project on the previous plan page.

Teacher & Pupil Assessment		Circle the stage that you think you have reached in each row, your teacher will check it.	
	Not used a count control loop	Used a count control loop to move a character	Used a count controlled loop to move a character and has used a count controlled loop independently for some other purpose
Count-controlled Loops	0 Marks	1 mark	2 marks
		Not used previous programming concepts for real purpose	Used previous programming concepts for real purpose
Used previous programming concept such as sequence and inputs		0 Marks	1 mark
	No theme in planning or code	Has a simple theme in planning or code	Has an interesting or amusing theme in planning or code
Has a project theme in planning or code	0 Marks	1 mark	2 marks

Come Back Doggy!
Predict Marksheet

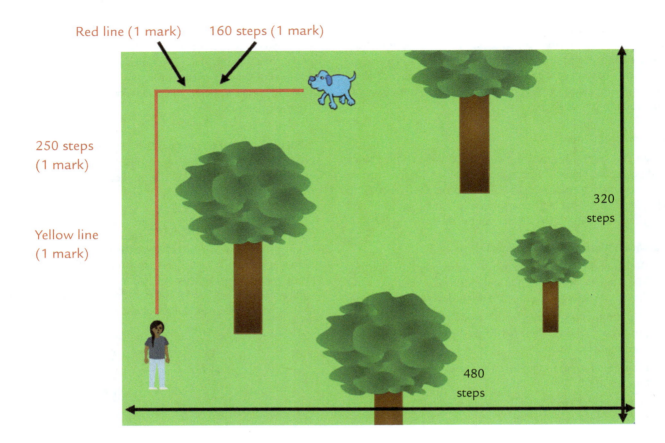

Red line (1 mark)   160 steps (1 mark)

250 steps
(1 mark)

Yellow line
(1 mark)

320 steps

480 steps

1. Draw a line where you think she will go first.
   (1 mark) for a line up from Maria as shown

2. Draw a line where you think she will go second.
   (1 mark) for a line across the top joining to first line as show above

3. Next to both lines write what colours you think they will be. *HINT Do not be put off by the American spelling of colour (color).*
   Yellow and then red marked on lines in correct places (2 marks)

4. Next to both lines write how many steps you think they will be.
   First line 250 steps, second line 160 steps (2 possible marks)

Come back doggy!
INVESTIGATE
Marksheet

Maria sprite questions

Maria

1. Which block starts the code?
   Green flag (1 mark)

2. What block makes Maria go back to the start? (Initialization) *HINT go to*
   go to x and y (1 mark)

3. Which block rubs out any old lines before Maria searches for her dog? (Initialization)
   Erase all (1 mark)

4. In the first repeat loop (count-controlled loop), how many times will move 1 step be run?
   250 (1 mark)

5. Which repeat loop draws the shortest line?
   Repeat 160 or the second repeat loop (1 mark)

6. Which block changes Maria's direction?
   Point in direction (1 mark)

Look at the code inside the dog
Dog Sprite Questions

7. Which line of code makes the dog wait until Maria arrives?
   Wait until touching Maria (1 mark)

8. Which blocks get repeated 21 times?
   Next costume (1 mark) wait 0.4 seconds (1 mark)

9. What direction (up, down, right or left) does point in direction 180 make the dog go?
   Down (1 mark)

Come Back Doggy!
CHANGE
Marksheet

Look at the code inside the Maria sprite
Make small changes to the code

Maria

1. Can you make Maria stop just before she touches the dog?
   What did you change? *HINT Repeat loop*

   Change repeat 160 to a number less than 130 (1 mark)

2. Can you make Maria bump into the tree after she catches up with the dog?
   What did you change? *HINT Repeat loop*

   Change repeat 160 to a number more than 220 (1 mark)

Look at the code inside the dog sprite
Make small changes to the code

3. Can you make the dog say something after the girl bumps into him?
   HINT Wait until touching…
   What code did you add? Add a say or sound block (1 mark)
   Where did you add it? Add it after the wait until touching Maria in either script (1 mark)

4. Can you make the dogs legs look like they are walking slower?
   What did you change?

   Change the wait inside the repeat 21 loop to a higher number such as 1 second (1 mark)

Come Back Doggy!
FLOW OF CONTROL ONLY

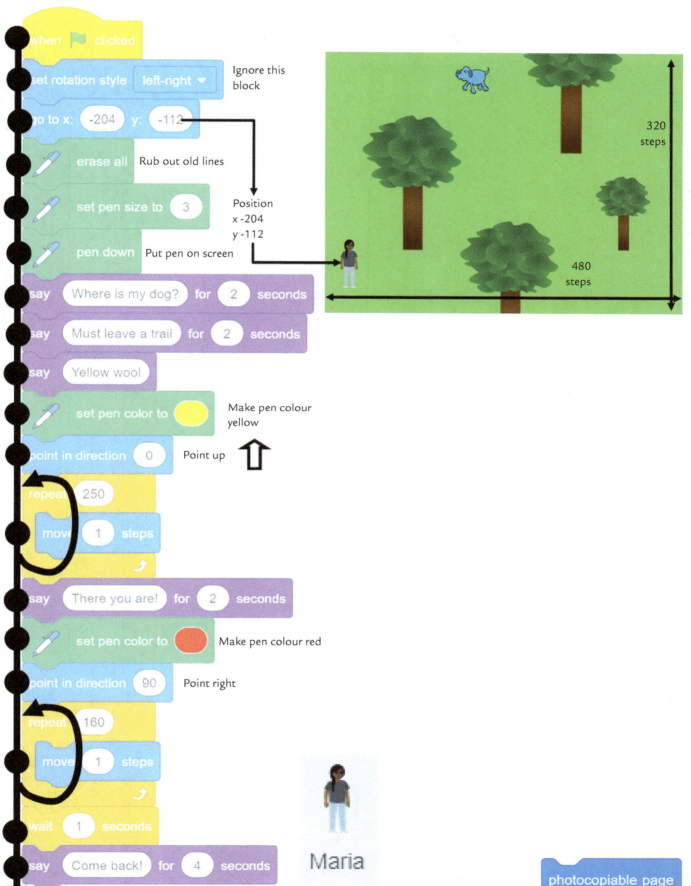

when ⚑ clicked

set rotation style left-right ▼   — Ignore this block

go to x: -204 y: -112   — Position x -204 y -112

erase all   Rub out old lines

set pen size to 3

pen down   Put pen on screen

say Where is my dog? for 2 seconds

say Must leave a trail for 2 seconds

say Yellow wool

set pen color to 🟡   Make pen colour yellow

point in direction 0   Point up ⬆

repeat 250
   move 1 steps

say There you are! for 2 seconds

set pen color to 🔴   Make pen colour red

point in direction 90   Point right

repeat 160
   move 1 steps

wait 1 seconds

say Come back! for 4 seconds

320 steps

480 steps

Maria

PROGRAMMING MODULES THAT USE INDEFINITE LOOPS

CHAPTER 6   Fish Tank

> **Overview**
> Pupils explore how Scratch can use an indefinite (forever) loop in a fish tank scene designed to amuse a younger brother or sister. Pupils then use these ideas to make their own scene for a younger sibling.

To do before the session

1. Look at the grid below and decide which optional and SEN activities you are going to include and exclude.
2. Print pupil worksheets for each activity chosen and staple into a booklet, one for each pupil.
3. Print marksheets for activities chosen to be placed where pupils can access them.
4. Download the code needed and place in a templates folder on your school network or add to a Scratch Studio or link on your learning platform.
5. Download the slides that go with the concept introduction.
6. Study the notes that go with the slides.
7. Examine the teacher help notes that are provided alongside every activity.

To do at the start of the session

If you have not introduced infinite indefinite loops with this class before do this first as a whole class activity.

To do after the concept has been introduced

Each activity has whole class notes to help you explain what is needed if it is the first time pupils have carried out this type of activity. There are also core instructions underneath in case you are sticking to the core activities only.

How this module fits into a programming progression

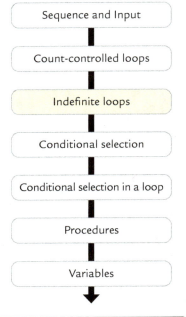

Sequence and Input

Count-controlled loops

Indefinite loops

Conditional selection

Conditional selection in a loop

Procedures

Variables

> **Vocabulary**
> Indefinite loop, Count-controlled loop, loop, repeat, do x times. Sprite, costume, backdrop, position, motion, degrees, direction, keyboard,

Resource Name	Core Optional SEN	Teacher	Pupil Grouping	How Assessed	SCRATCH ACCESS
CONCEPT Indefinite Loop	CORE	Leads Session	Solo whole class activity	Formative	NO
PARSONS	OPTIONAL SEN OPTIONAL ALL (predict or parsons not both)	Support Poor Readers	Solo or Paired (Teacher choice)	Pupil Marked Marksheet Provided	YES Fish Tank Parsons
FLOW	OPTIONAL ALL	Support Poor Readers	Solo or Paired (Teacher Choice)	Pupil Marked Marksheet Provided	NO
PREDICT	OPTIONAL ALL (predict or parsons not both)	Support Poor Readers	Paired	Pupil Marked Marksheet Provided	NO
INVESTIGATE	CORE	Support Poor Readers	Paired	Pupil Marked Marksheet Provided	YES Fish Tank
CHANGE	CORE	Support Poor Readers	Paired	Pupil Marked Marksheet Provided	YES Fish Tank
CREATE	CORE	Assesses pupil work and checks pupil self-assessment	Solo	Pupil Assessed & Teacher Assessed	YES Fish Tank Wild animals space scene dinosaur

(Yellow is core module, pink and white are optional.)

Core activities general instructions

1. Group pupils in roughly same ability pairs. For **investigate** and **change** worksheets, pupils will work in pairs, for **create** they will work separately.

2. Give out the pupil booklets and explain that pupils need to follow the instructions on the sheets to explore how **indefinite-loops** work.

3. Explain that each pupil will record separately whilst working alongside their partner and keeping to the same pace as their partner.

4. Demonstrate where they can find the template code and explain that pupils will share one device for investigate and change.

5. Explain that during each question only one person should touch the shared device and they should swap who that person is when there is a new questions.

6. Encourage them to discuss their answers with their partner. If they disagree with their partner, they can record a different answer in their own booklet.

7. Show pupils where it says they should mark their work on the sheet where the answer sheets are in the classroom.

8. Remind pupils to return marksheets after marking because there are not enough for every pair to have their own.

Key Programming Knowledge

A **loop** is any set of instructions that are repeated
An **algorithm** is any set of instructions to carry out a task that can be understood by another human
Decomposing is breaking a problem down into smaller parts and solving each part separately

An (infinite) indefinite loop

Can replace a sequence where there is a pattern
Only ends when the digital device is turned off
Is called an indefinite loop because we do not know how many times it will repeat
Is called a forever loop in Scratch programming
Has a flow of control (order that commands are run in)
Can be used in an algorithm or in programming

Resources

Fish Tank Template   https://scratch.mit.edu/projects/509454779/editor/
Fish Tank Parsons   https://scratch.mit.edu/projects/621604368/
https://scratch.mit.edu/projects/510616705/ (wild animals)
https://scratch.mit.edu/projects/510619599/ (space scene)
https://scratch.mit.edu/projects/510620349/ (dinosaurs)

	On the sheet, if it says no Scratch, they must work only on the sheet.
	If it says Scratch with a green tick, they can use one device between the pair.
	If it says work with a partner, they must work at the same speed as their partner.
	If it says work on their own, they must do this using a separate device each working alone.

English Computing National Curriculum Programs of Study

Pupils should be taught to:

- **design, write and debug programs that accomplish specific goals**, including controlling or simulating physical systems; **solve problems by decomposing them into smaller parts.**

- **use sequence**, selection and **repetition in programs**; work with variables **and various forms of input and output.**

- **use logical reasoning to explain how some simple algorithms work and to detect and correct errors in algorithms and programs.**

Scottish Curriculum for Excellence Technologies

I understand the instructions of a visual programming language and can predict the outcome of a program written using the language. TCH 1-14a

I can explain core programming language concepts in appropriate technical language TCH 2-14a

I can demonstrate a range of basic problem solving skills by building simple programs to carry out a given task, using an appropriate language. TCH 1-15a

I can create, develop and evaluate computing solutions in response to a design challenge. TCH 2-15a

Welsh National Curriculum Relevant Strands

Progression Step 3.

- I can identify repeating patterns and use loops to make my algorithms more concise.

- I can explain and debug algorithms.

FISH TANK PARSONS

**Start Scratch and load
FISH TANK PARSONS**

All the code has been selected but some of it in the app is unconnected. Use the algorithms below to help you connect the code.

Start on green flag

Go to x and y

Rotate left right only

Point right (90)

Loop always

    Move a step

    If touch edge of screen bounce

Start on green flag

Go behind a layer

Go to x and y

Rotate left right only

Point down (180)

Loop always

    Move half a step

    If touch edge of screen bounce

Start on green flag

Loop always

    Change costume

    Pause a second

An **algorithm** is any set of instructions to carry out a task that can be understood by another human. An algorithm can be used to plan programming

Now check your answers to see if they are correct using the Parsons marksheet

photocopiable page

SUPPORT PARSONS

Start Scratch and load FISH TANK PARSONS

All the code has been selected but some of it in the app is unconnected. Use the algorithms below to help you connect the code.

Start on green flag
Go to x and y
Rotate left right only
Point right (90)
Loop always
    Move a step
    If touch edge of screen bounce

Start on green flag
Go behind a layer
Go to x and y
Rotate left right only
Point down (180)
Loop always
    Move half a step
    If touch edge of screen bounce

Start on green flag
Loop always
    Change costume
    Pause a second

Notes on the activity

This allows pupils to build part of the code first before investigating, modifying and creating code of their own. The algorithm is written in language similar but also different to the code. This helps pupils by enabling them to see an example of planning which will help them when they come to plan their own project. On its own it is not enough deep thinking about the code to enable agency but as a starter or SEN activity it is useful to see how code can be built.

Whole class advice

Load fish tank Parsons code and then use the algorithm on this page to build the code. When you have completed it, run the code and check your answer with the marking sheet.

Send advice

Parsons problems can be made less complex by connecting more blocks in the example Scratch code and saving that version as a new template.

Understanding programming

You can find out more about Parsons problems in the teacher book, Chapter 19.

Individual advice

Pointing out that the code inside the loop is indented in the planning algorithm can help some pupils.

Individual advice Jellyfish

Pointing out that as there are two algorithms there will be two sections of code.

Now check your answers to see if they are correct using the Parsons marksheet

Fish Tank Scene
FLOW

Work with a partner

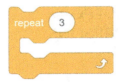

indefinite loop

1. Find the forever loops in the code. Put a star *
   on every block of code inside the forever loops.

2. Draw a line to show the order the code will be
   run in on the other code. Draw dots to show
   actions. The Jellyfish has been done for you.

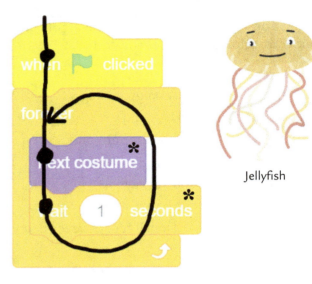

Jellyfish

Now mark this sheet using the answer sheet

photocopiable page

A

Supporting FLOW

Whole class instructions

Look at this code carefully. Now draw the flow of control on top of the code as a line and each action as a dot. Be sure you know where the indefinite forever loop is.

1. Find the forever loops in the code. Put a star * on every block of code inside the forever loops.

2. Draw a line to show the order the code will be run in on the other code. Draw dots to show actions. The Jellyfish has been done for you.

Notes on the activity

This could be a lesson starter type activity or part of the predict or investigate process or saved for pupils who struggled to answer questions about loops.

If using it as a lesson starter, get all pupils to trace the flow of control over the Jellyfish example with you. Point out that forever is where the loop starts. They could then complete one of the other examples, so you can check any pupils who struggle. You can then mark that example with the class before completing the last example.

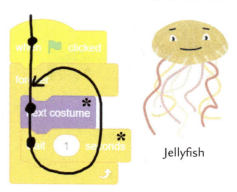

Jellyfish

Say

Remember the line shows the order that the code will run in and the dots mark actions that will happen. There is an example at the top and we drew some when we introduced indefinite loop algorithms.

Individual support

Most pupils can draw the flow of control for these, but making sure they really understand how the loop works is harder.

Ask them to say the actions as they happen. If they continue around the loop more than once, you know they understand how the loop really works.

Go to x and y

set rotation style

point direction 90

move 1

If on edge bounce

move 1

If on edge bounce

move 1

If on edge bounce,

etc.

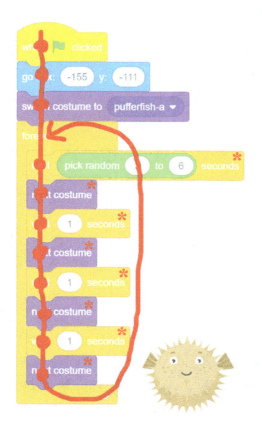

Does the line start at the top and loop back where the forever loop starts? (1 mark)

Are all the dots on the line? (1 mark)

Are their stars on every block inside the loop? (1 mark)

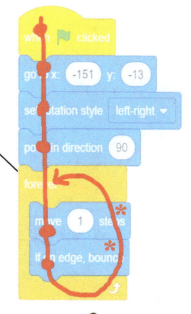

Does the line start at the top and loop back where the forever loop starts? (1 mark)

Are all the dots on the line? (1 mark)

Are their stars on every block inside the loop? (1 mark)

Now mark this sheet using the answer sheet

Remind pupils to mark this sheet before moving on and to tell you if they got them all wrong, so you can help.

Fish Tank Scene
PREDICT

Read the code and any pictures near it. Predict what each script will do when started. Do not copy the text in the blocks in your prediction. Focus on the code inside the forever or repeat loops.

Work with a partner

Don't load Scratch

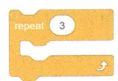

indefinite loop

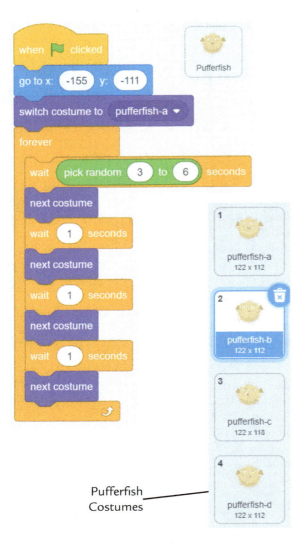

Pufferfish Costumes

I predict that when this code is run the pufferfish will

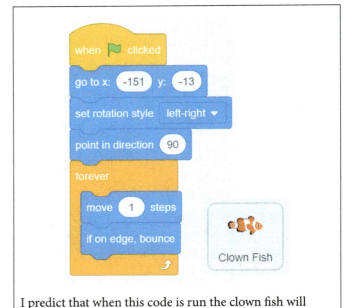

Clown Fish

I predict that when this code is run the clown fish will

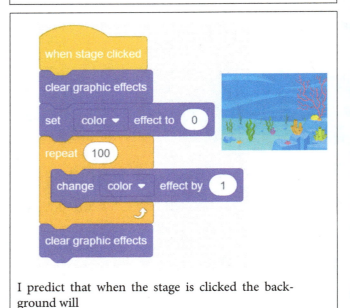

I predict that when the stage is clicked the background will

Now mark predict using the answer sheet

photocopiable page

Supporting PREDICT

Read the code and any pictures near it. Predict what each script will do when started. Do not copy the text in the blocks in your prediction. Focus on the code inside the forever or repeat loops.

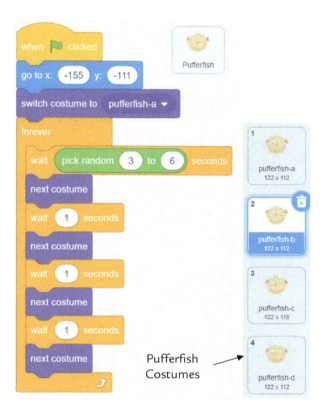

Pufferfish Costumes

I predict the when this code is run the pufferfish will change its facial expressions.

(1 mark for any indication that its face or how it looks or the costumes will change)

Notes on the activity

This optional activity helps pupils to think about the bigger purpose of the program before they start looking at parts of it in later sections.

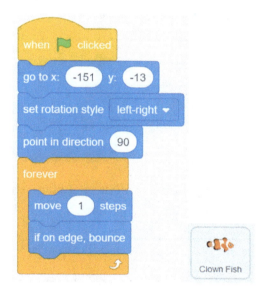

I predict that when this code is run the clown fish will move across the screen and bounce of the sides.

(1 mark for any indication of moving and bouncing)

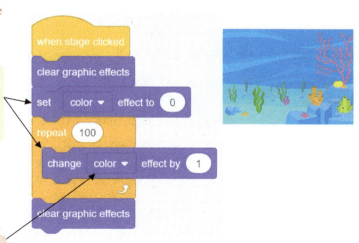

I predict that when the stage is clicked the background will change colour.

(1 mark for any indication of colour changing)

Fish Tank Scene
INVESTIGATE

Start Scratch and load
Fish Tank Life

Work with a partner

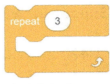

indefinite loop

Run the code
Play the Fish Tank Life scene a few times.

Investigate the Code
Run the programs lots of times to help you answer the questions but don't change the code.

Look at the code inside the Clown Fish

Clown Fish Sprite Questions

1. Name the blocks that are inside the forever (indefinite) loop?

   A_____

   B_____

2. What direction does the Clown Fish set off in?

   _____

3. How many times will move 1 step be run?

   A 90 times   B Once   C 10 times   D We don't know

   _____

Look at the code inside Pufferfish

Pufferfish Sprite Questions

4. How many times will the **change color effect by 10** be run when the sprite is clicked?

5. When the code gets to **wait pick random 3 to 6 seconds** circle all the seconds it might have to wait

   A   3 or 6 seconds

   B   6 seconds

   C   3, 4, 5 or 6 seconds

   D   3 seconds

Now mark the investigate questions using the answer sheet

photocopiable page

Supporting INVESTIGATE

Run the code

Play the Fish Tank Life scene a few times.

Investigate the code

Run the programs lots of times to help you answer the questions but don't change the code

Look at the code inside the Clown Fish

Clown Fish Sprite Questions

1. Name the blocks that are inside the forever (indefinite) loop?

   A move 1 step (1 mark)

   B if on edge, bounce (1 mark)

2. What direction does the Clown Fish set off in?

   90 degrees or to the right (1 mark)

3. How many times will move 1 step be run?

   A 90 times   B Once
   C 10 times   D We don't know

   D We don't know (1 mark)

Look at the code inside Pufferfish

Pufferfish Sprite Questions

4. How many times will the **change color effect by 10** be run when the sprite is clicked?

   100 times (1 mark)

5. When the code gets to **wait pick random 3 to 6 seconds** circle all the seconds it might have to wait

   A   3 or 6 seconds

   B   6 seconds

   C   3, 4, 5 or 6 seconds   (1 mark)

   D   3 seconds

Now mark the investigate questions using the answer sheet

Notes on the activity

Investigating the code encourages pupils to think deeply about how it works. Check that every pupil is filling in and marking the questions individually but at the pace of the slowest in the pair. Sometimes a pair decides not to mark to speed up their efforts. Marking gives valuable information, so I recommend sending them back to mark their work. A class instruction to come and talk to you if they have over half of the questions wrong or they do not understand the answer after they have marked it helps to check progress is being made correctly. There is real value in collecting these scores to build up a summative picture of pupil progress.

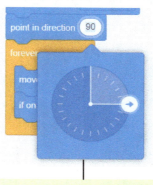

Q2 Encourage pupils who are stuck on this one to click on the 90 in the point in direction block.

Q3 Explain that the indefinite (forever) loop will carry on until someone stops the program, but this could be at any time.

Q3 We could use a variable to see how many times it is run, but that would be beyond most primary pupils at this point.

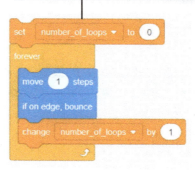

Q4 This question is here to revise count-controlled loops from previous modules.

Q5 Ask pupils to count every time the fish changes direction. Is it the same amount each time? Is it always 3 or 6 seconds?

Fish Tank Scene
CHANGE

Work with a partner

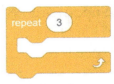
indefinite loop

**Start Scratch and load the
Come Fish Tank Life program**

Make small changes to the code

Clown Fish Sprite Question

1. Can you make the Clown Fish swim faster?

   What did you change?

Jellyfish Sprite Question

2. Can you make the Jellyfish swim in a
   different direction?

   What did you change?

Blue Fish Questions

3. Can you make the Blue Fish change direction
   every 4 seconds?

   What did you change?

Pufferfish Sprite Question

4. Can you make the Pufferfish wait for 5 to 10 seconds
   before changing costumes?

   What did you change?

Stage Question

5. Can you make the stage end on a red background when it is
   clicked? *HINT You might need to remove a block as
   well as change a number*

   What did you change?

Now mark the changing code questions using the answer sheet

photocopiable page

D

Supporting CHANGE

Make small changes to the code

Clown Fish Sprite Question

1. Can you make the Clown Fish swim faster?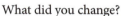

   What did you change?

   Change move 1 step to a higher number (1 mark)

Jellyfish Sprite Question

2. Can you make the Jellyfish swim in a different direction?

   What did you change?

   Change the point in direction to any number other than 180 (1 mark)

Blue Fish Questions

3. Can you make the Blue Fish change direction every 4 seconds?

   What did you change?

   Either remove pick random and change wait to 4 seconds for both wait blocks or change pick random to 4 to 4 (1 mark)

Pufferfish Sprite Question

4. Can you make the Pufferfish wait for 5 to 10 seconds before changing costumes?

   What did you change?

   Change wait pick random to 5 to 10 seconds (1 mark)

Stage Question

5. Can you make the stage end on a red background when it is clicked? *HINT You might need to remove a block as well as change a number*

   What did you change?

   Change repeat loop to 70 or similar number (1 mark) and remove clear graphic effect from the end (1 mark)

Now mark the Change questions using the answer sheet

Notes on the activity

Changing or modifying code is a core part of this module, so I suggest you do not leave it out. It is an important step towards creation of their own code, as parts they have modified they will feel more ownership of. Recording marks will help with assessment.

Send advice

Support pairs of pupils who are poor readers by reading questions, reading code samples and covering up questions until they get to them.

Q1 HINT Swimming is moving. I wonder which block controls moving?

Q2 HINT What is the keyword you can find in the question and the code? Direction.

Whole class support

Apart from the last question you will only need to change a number to answer each question. If you change it and it does not do what you want, remember to change it back before examining another option.

Q3 & 4 You can give pupils the random card resource to help them answer these questions.

Q4 The best way to explain pick random is with a dice. You can simulate a dice with pick random 1 to 6.

Q4 Some pupils will not realize that there can be code in the stage area, so pointing out that clicking on the stage icon to show the code will help.

Q5 Color (US Spelling) is a system variable. Any code that has a set and change block is also a system variable. Most pupils will not be ready for this concept yet.

Q5 If pupils are struggling for time, Question 5 is a good question to remove so that they get creative make time in the next section.

Whole class support

Remind pupils to mark the changing code questions and to report any answers that they still do not understand. It is far easier for a teacher to help at this point than after the lesson.

Fish Tank Scene
CREATE

Work on
your own

indefinite loop

Choose One Option

Option 1

Plan and code a moving scene with wild animals

Use Wild Animals Template

Option 2

Plan and code a moving scene with pets

Option 3

Plan and code a moving space scene

Use Space Template

Option 4

Plan and code a moving scene with dinosaurs

Use Wild Dinosaur Template

Option 5

Plan and code your own moving scene

Fish Tank Life was made for a very young child to explore. Your scene must also be made for a younger audience.

- You must use forever loops for a real purposes.
- You will get extra marks if you use count-controlled loops.
- You will get extra marks if your theme is easily recognized.
- You will lose marks if you make a game.
- You will lose marks if you use lots of text.

You can use the templates as a starting place or choose your own sprites and backgrounds.

> My moving scene theme will be

> My moving scene characters and backgrounds

> My moving scene plan Where will characters start? Where will they move (arrows)? Will there be things to click on?

Teacher & Pupil Assessment   Circle the stage that you think you have reached in each row. Your teacher will check it.

	Not used a forever loop	Copied a forever loop from the fish tank project	Copied and changed a forever loop idea	Used a forever loop in a way not shown
Indefinite (forever) loops	0 marks	1 mark	2 marks	3 marks

		Not used previous programming concepts for real purpose	Used previous programming concepts for real purpose
Used previous programming concept such as count-controlled loops		0 marks	1 mark

		No theme in planning or code	Has a theme in planning or code
Has a project theme in planning or code		0 marks	1 mark

You can check your progress using the planning and making code marksheet

photocopiable page

Supporting CREATE

Choose one option

Option 1
Plan and code a moving scene with wild animals.

Option 2
Plan and code a moving scene with pets.

Option 3
Plan and code a moving space scene.

Option 4
Plan and code a moving scene with dinosaurs.

Option 5
Plan and code your own moving scene.

My moving scene characters and backgrounds

Have pupils identified characters and backgrounds that go with their theme?

Whole class support

Towards the end of the module, ask pupils to self-assess their work using the three rows at the bottom. Use of indefinite (forever) loops, project theme and use of previous concepts.

Notes on the activity

The make part of a project is really important, and teachers should always make sure that pupils have time to make their own project, even if that means reducing the time spent on other stages for pupils who work slowly. It helps if pupils work on their own for this while supporting their partner.

Things to check

Is your project made for a young child?

Has it used forever loops for a real purposes

Has it used a use count-controlled loop?

Is the theme is easily recognized?

Have you made a game? (minus 1 mark)

Has it got lots of text? (minus 1 mark)

My moving scene theme will be

Have pupils identified one of the options above or chosen their own option?

Marking planning is a great way of valuing planning. You may not want to mark planning every time, but it is useful to do on occasions.

My moving scene plan

Where will characters start?

Where will they move (arrows)?

Will there be things to click on?

Warn pupils that you are going to start assessing their work. It is easier to assess during the lesson when you can ask questions about their work and pupils can answer these. Start assessing before the end of the module, so that pupils can improve their work and come back for a final assessment. Start with pupils who started their final phase earlier to give late finishers the most amount of time.

Teacher & Pupil Assessment   Circle the stage that you think you have reached in each row. Your teacher will check it.

	Not used a forever loop	Copied a forever loop from the fish tank project	Copied and changed a forever loop idea	Used a forever loop in a way not shown
Indefinite (forever) loops	0 marks	1 mark	2 marks	3 marks

Look to see if they have use a count-controlled loop meaningfully		Not used previous programming concepts for real purpose	Used previous programming concepts for real purpose
Used previous programming concept such as count-controlled loops		0 marks	1 mark

		No theme in planning or code	Has a theme in planning or code
Has a project theme in planning or code		0 marks	1 mark

FLOW Marksheet

1. Find the forever loops in the code. Put a star *
   on every block of code inside the forever loops.

2. Draw a line to show the order the code will be
   run in on the other code. Draw dots to show
   actions.

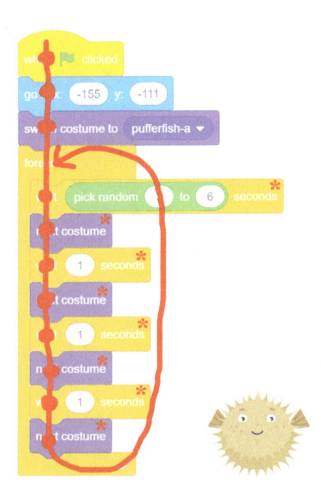

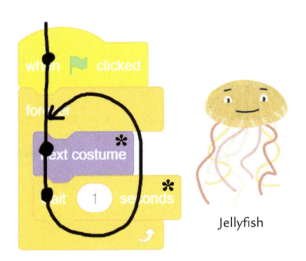

Jellyfish

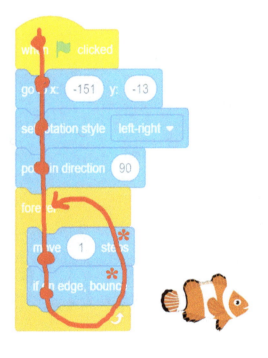

Does the line start at the top and loop back where
the forever loop starts? (1 mark)

Are all the dots on the line? (1 mark)

Are their stars on every block inside the loop? (1
mark)

Does the line start at the top and loop back where
the forever loop starts? (1 mark)

Are all the dots on the line? (1 mark)

Are their stars on every block inside the loop? (1
mark)

photocopiable page

Fish Tank Life
PREDICT

Marksheet

Read the code and any pictures near it. Predict what each script will do when started. Do not copy the text in the blocks in your prediction. Focus on the code inside the forever or repeat loops.

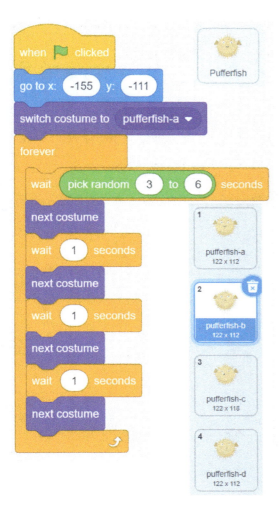

I predict that when this code is run, the pufferfish will change its facial expressions.

(1 mark for any indication that its face or how it looks or the costumes will change)

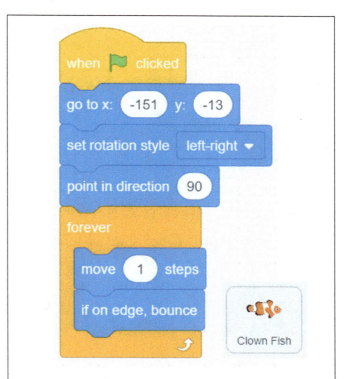

I predict that when this code is run, the clown fish will move across the screen and bounce of the sides.

(1 mark for any indication of moving and bouncing)

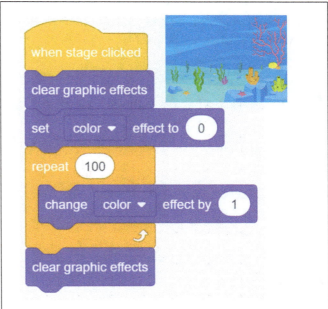

I predict that when the stage is clicked the background will change colour.

(1 mark for any indication of colour changing)

photocopiable page

Fish Tank Life
INVESTIGATE

Marksheet

Investigate the Code
Run the programs lot of times to help you answer the questions but don't change the code.

Look at the code inside the Clown Fish

Clown Fish Sprite Questions

1. Name the blocks that are inside the forever (indefinite) loop?
    A move 1 step (1 mark)
    B if on edge, bounce (1 mark)

2. What direction does the Clown Fish set off in?
    90 degrees or to the right (1 mark)

3. How many times will move 1 step be run?
    A 90 times   B Once   C 10 times   D We don't know
    D We don't know (1 mark)

Look at the code inside Pufferfish

Pufferfish Sprite Questions
4. How many times will the **change colour effect by 10** be run when the sprite is clicked?
    100 times (1 mark)

5. When the code gets to **wait pick random 3 to 6 seconds** circle all the seconds it might have to wait
    A   3 or 6 seconds
    B   6 seconds
    C   3, 4, 5 or 6 seconds (1 mark)
    D   3 seconds

photocopiable page

H

Fish Tank Life
CHANGE

Marksheet

Make small changes to the code

Clown Fish Sprite Question

1. Can you make the Clown Fish swim faster?

    What did you change?

    Change move 1 step to a higher number (1 mark)

Jellyfish Sprite Question

2. Can you make the Jellyfish swim in a different direction?

    What did you change?

    Change the point in direction to any number other than 180 (1 mark)

Blue Fish Questions

3. Can you make the Blue Fish change direction every 4 seconds?

    What did you change?

    Either remove pick random and change wait to 4 seconds
    for both wait blocks or change pick random to 4 to 4 (1 mark)

Pufferfish Sprite Question

4. Can you make the Pufferfish wait for 5 to 10 seconds before
    changing costumes?

    What did you change?

    Change wait pick random to 5 to 10 seconds (1 mark)

Stage Question

5. Can you make the stage end on a red background when it is clicked?
    HINT You might need to remove a block as well as change a number.

    What did you change?

    Change repeat loop to 70 or similar number (1 mark) and remove
    clear graphic effect from the end (1 mark)

Fish Tank Life
CREATE

HELP SHEET

Things to check

Is your project made for a young child? (1 mark)

Has it used forever loops for a real purpose? (1 mark)

Has it used a use count-controlled loop? (1 mark)

Is the theme easily recognized? (1 mark)

Have you made a game? (minus 1 mark)

Has it got lots of text? (minus 1 mark)

My moving scene theme will be

Have pupils identified one of the options above or chosen their own option? (1mark)

My moving scene characters and backgrounds

Have pupils identified characters and backgrounds that go with their theme? (1 mark)

My moving scene plan

Where will characters start? (1 mark)

Where will they move (arrows)? (1 mark)

Will there be things to click on? (1 mark)

Teacher & Pupil Assessment Circle the stage that you think you have reached in each row, your teacher will check it.

Have you used indefinite (forever loops) for real purposes? (1-3 marks)	Not used a forever loop	Copied a forever loop from the fish tank project	Copied and changed a forever loop idea	Used a forever loop in a way not shown
Indefinite (forever) loops	0 Marks	1 mark	2 marks	3 marks

Have you used a count-controlled loop meaningfully (1 mark)		Not used previous programming concepts for real purpose	Used previous programming concepts for real purpose
Used previous programming concept such as count-controlled loops		0 Marks	1 mark

Have you stuck to a theme? (1mark)		No theme in planning or code	Has a theme in planning or code
Has a project theme in planning or code		0 Marks	1 mark

Have you circled where you are on each row?

photocopiable page

J

Overview
Pupils explore how Scratch can use an indefinite (forever) loop in a Helicopter game. Pupils then use these ideas to make their own simple game using indefinite (forever) loops.

To do before the session

1. Look at the grid below and decide which optional and SEN activities you are going to include and exclude.
2. Print pupil worksheets for each activity chosen and staple into a booklet, one for each pupil.
3. Print marksheets for activities chosen to be placed where pupils can access them.
4. Download the code needed and place in a templates folder on your school network or add to a Scratch Studio or link on your learning platform.
5. Download the slides that go with the concept introduction.
6. Study the notes that go with the slides.
7. Examine the teacher help notes that are provided alongside every activity.

To do at the start of the session

If you have not introduced infinite indefinite loops with this class before, do this first as a whole class activity.

To do after the concept has been introduced

Each activity has whole class notes to help you explain what is needed if it is the first time pupils have carried out this type of activity. There are also core instructions underneath in case you are sticking to the core activities only.

How this module fits into a programming progression

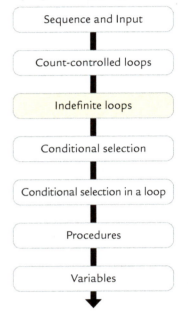

Vocabulary
Indefinite loop, count-controlled loop, loop, repeat, do x times, sprite, costume, backdrop, position, motion, degrees, direction, keyboard

Resource Name	Core Optional SEN	Teacher	Pupil Grouping	How Assessed	SCRATCH ACCESS
CONCEPT Indefinite Loop	CORE	Leads Session	Solo whole class activity	Formative	NO
PARSONS	OPTIONAL SEN OPTIONAL ALL (predict or parsons not both)	Support Poor Readers	Solo or Paired (Teacher choice)	Pupil Marked Marksheet Provided	YES Helicopter Game Parsons
FLOW	OPTIONAL ALL	Support Poor Readers	Solo or Paired (Teacher Choice)	Pupil Marked Marksheet Provided	NO
PREDICT	OPTIONAL ALL	Support Poor Readers	Paired	Pupil Marked Marksheet Provided	NO
INVESTIGATE	CORE	Support Poor Readers	Paired	Pupil Marked Marksheet Provided	YES Helicopter Game
CHANGE	CORE	Support Poor Readers	Paired	Pupil Marked Marksheet Provided	YES Helicopter Game
CREATE	CORE	Assesses pupil work and checks pupil self-assessment	Solo	Pupil Assessed & Teacher Assessed	YES Helicopter Game

(Yellow is core module, pink and white are optional.)

Core activities general instructions

1. Group pupils in roughly same ability pairs. For **investigate** and **change** worksheets, pupils will work in pairs, for **create** they will work separately.

2. Give out the pupil booklets and explain that pupils need to follow the instructions on the sheets to explore how **indefinite-loops** work.

3. Explain that each pupil will record separately while working alongside their partner and keeping to the same pace as their partner

4. Demonstrate where they can find the template code and explain that pupils will share one device for investigate and change.

5. Explain that during each question only one person should touch the shared device and they should swap who that person is when there is a new questions.

6. Encourage them to discuss their answers with their partner. If they disagree with their partner, they can record a different answer in their own booklet.

7. Show pupils where it says they should mark their work on the sheet and where the answer sheets are in the classroom.

8. Remind pupils to return marksheets after marking, because there are not enough for every pair to have their own.

Key Programming Knowledge

A **loop** is any set of instructions that are repeated

An **algorithm** is any set of instructions to carry out a task that can be understood by another human

Decomposing is breaking a problem down into smaller parts and solving each part separately

An (infinite) indefinite loop

Can replace a sequence where there is a pattern

Only ends when the digital device is turned off

Is called an indefinite loop because we do not know how many times it will repeat

Is called a forever loop in Scratch programming

Has a flow of control (order that commands are run in)

Can be used in an algorithm or in programming

Resources

Helicopter	https://scratch.mit.edu/projects/316961043/
Helicopter Parsons	https://scratch.mit.edu/projects/316961377/

	On the sheet, if it says no Scratch, they must work only on the sheet,
	If it says Scratch with a green tick, they can use one device between the pair.
	If it says work with a partner, they must work at the same speed as their partner.
	If it says work on their own, they must do this using a separate device each working alone.

English Computing National Curriculum Programs of Study

Pupils should be taught to:

- **design, write and debug programs that accomplish specific goals**, including controlling or simulating physical systems; solve problems by decomposing them into smaller parts

- **use sequence**, selection and **repetition in programs**; work with variables **and various forms of input and output**

- **use logical reasoning to explain how some simple algorithms work and to detect and correct errors in algorithms and programs**

Scottish Curriculum for Excellence Technologies

I understand the instructions of a visual programming language and can predict the outcome of a program written using the language. TCH 1-14a

I can explain core programming language concepts in appropriate technical language TCH 2-14a

I can demonstrate a range of basic problem solving skills by building simple programs to carry out a given task, using an appropriate language. TCH 1-15a

I can create, develop and evaluate computing solutions in response to a design challenge. TCH 2-15a

Welsh National Curriculum Relevant Strands

Progression Step 3.

- I can identify repeating patterns and use loops to make my algorithms more concise.

- I can explain and debug algorithms.

Helicopter Game
PARSONS

Start Scratch and load
Helicopter parsons

Look in the helicopter sprite

All the correct code is there, but it needs assembling in the right order.

Use the algorithm below to help you assemble it.

Green flag start
Loop always
    Helicopter costume 2
    Pause tenth of second
    Helicopter costume 3
    Pause tenth of second
    Helicopter costume 4
    Pause tenth of second
	Green flag start
	Go X –159 Y –131
	3 secs move to X –74 Y113
	Loop always
	    Point to mouse cursor
	    Move one step

Green flag start
Stop drawing pen up
Clear all lines
Pause 3 seconds
Start drawing pen down
Pen size 3
Loop always
    Pen colour light grey
    Pause 1 second
    Pen colour dark grey
    Pause 1 second
	Green flag start
	Pause three seconds
	Say mayday for two seconds
	Say Helicopter in trouble for two seconds
	Say avoid the birds for two seconds

An **algorithm** is any set of instructions to carry out a task that can be understood by another human. An algorithm can be used to plan programming.

Use the Parsons marksheet to check your work

photocopiable page

Supporting PARSONS

Whole class advice

Load helicopter Parsons code and then use the algorithm on this page to build the code. When you have completed it, run the code and check your answer with the marking sheet.

Understanding programming

You can find out more about Parsons problems in the teacher book, Chapter19.

Individual advice

Pointing out that the code affected by the condition is indented once, that it is in the if block and it is indented in the planning algorithm, can help some pupils.

Notes on the activity

This allows pupils to build part of the code first before investigating, modifying and creating code of their own. The algorithm is written in language similar but also different to the code. This helps pupils by enabling them to see an example of planning which will help them when they come to plan their own project. On its own it is not enough deep thinking about the code to enable agency, but as a starter or SEN activity it is useful to see how code can be built.

Able advice

Parsons problems can be made more complex by separating more blocks in the example Scratch code and adding a few extra unnecessary blocks before saving that version as a new template.

Send advice

Parsons problems can be made less complex by connecting more blocks in the example Scratch code and saving that version as a new template.

Look in the helicopter sprite.

All the correct code is there, but it needs assembling in the right order.

Use the algorithm below to help you assemble it.

Green flag start	Green flag start	Green flag start	Green flag start
Loop always	Go X –159 Y –131	Stop drawing pen up	Pause three seconds
Helicopter costume 2	3 secs move to X –74 Y113	Clear all lines	Say mayday for two seconds
Pause tenth of second	Loop always	Pause 3 seconds	Say Helicopter in trouble for two seconds
Helicopter costume 3	Point to mouse cursor	Start drawing pen down	Say avoid the birds for two seconds
Pause tenth of second	Move one step	Pen size 3	
Helicopter costume 4		Loop always	
Pause tenth of second		Pen colour light grey	
		Pause 1 second	
		Pen colour dark grey	
		Pause 1 second	

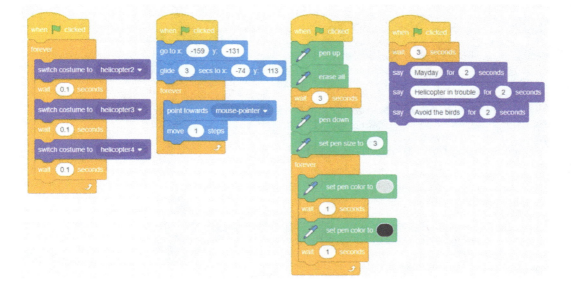

Helicopter game
FLOW

Work with a partner

Don't load
Scratch

indefinite loop

1. Find the forever loop and tick all the blocks inside the loop.
2. Draw a line to show the order the code will be run in. Draw dots to show actions. One has been done for you.

Example

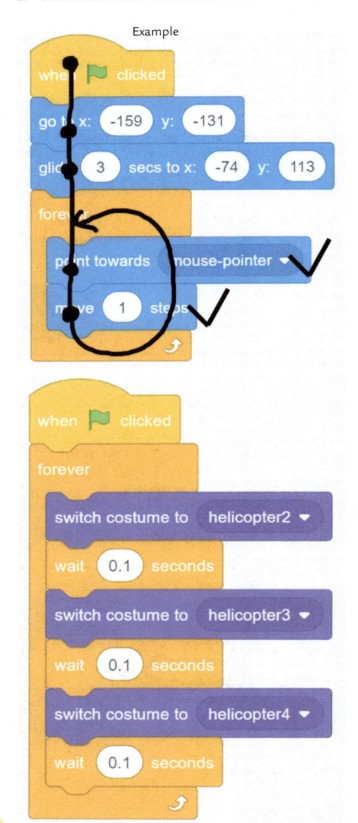

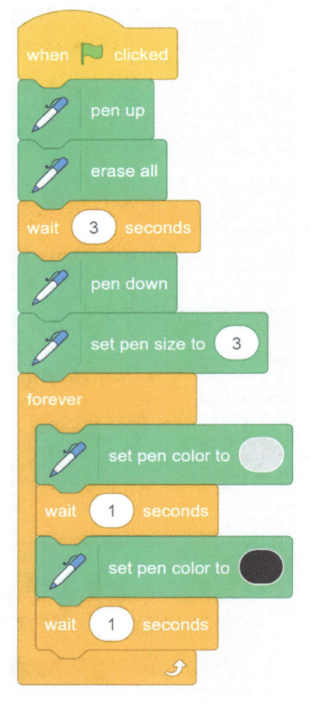

Now mark this sheet using the answer sheet

photocopiable page

Supporting FLOW

1. Find the forever loop and tick all the blocks inside the loop.
2. Draw a line to show the order the code will be run in. Draw dots to show actions. One has been done for you.

Notes on the activity

This activity builds on the concept introduction and could be completed directly after it instead of in the order provided here. It could also be used to work with SEN pupils only.

Whole class instructions

Remember, the line shows the order that the code will run in and the dots mark actions that will happen. There is an example at the top right and we drew some when we introduced indefinite loop algorithms

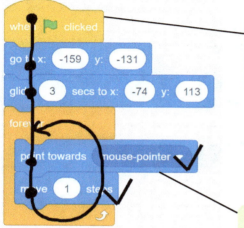

If a pupil is stuck read the example code and at the same time trace your finger over the example flow. Make sure you go around the loop a couple of times.

Most pupils can draw the flow of control for these, but making sure they really understand how the loop works is harder.

Ask them to say the actions as they happen. If they continue around the loop more than once, you know they understand how the loop really works.

Go to x and y

Glide to x and y

Point towards mouse move 1 step

Point towards mouse

Move 1 step,

etc.

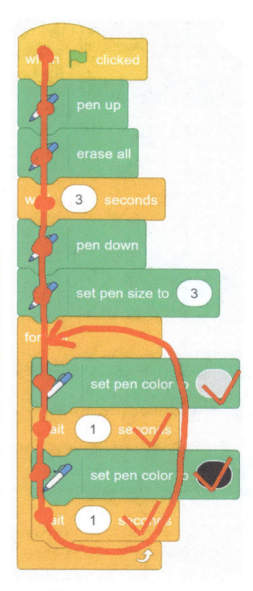

(1 mark) for the loop drawn as shown
(1 mark) for the dots drawn as shown
(1 mark) for all the ticks

(1 mark) for the loop drawn as shown
(1 mark) for the dots drawn as shown
(1 mark) for all the ticks

Now mark this sheet using the answer sheet

Helicopter game
PREDICT

Don't load Scratch

Work with a partner

indefinite loop

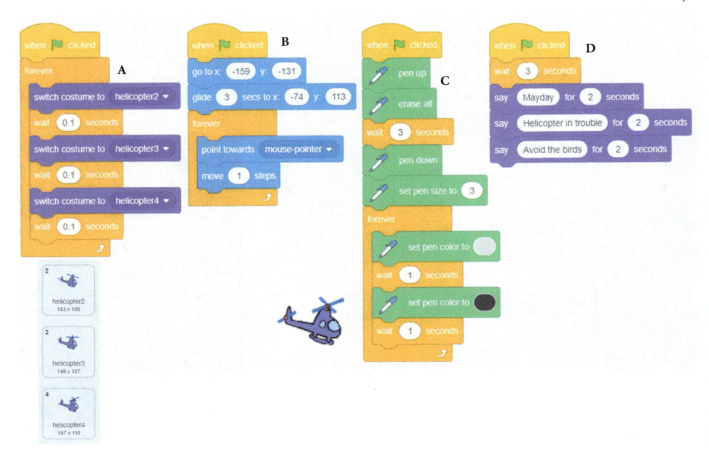

Reading code

1. How many forever (indefinite) loops are in all of the helicopter code above?

2. What code blocks are inside the forever (indefinite) loop in code block B?

3. How many seconds will code block D run for once the green flag is clicked?

4. How long does it stay light grey for before changing to dark grey in code block C?

Match the code block to the correct prediction. The first one has been done for you.

Read the main program code sections A to D slowly from top to bottom. Beware, there are two false predictions which don't match any code above!

D					
Say what has happened to the helicopter and what the user should do in the game.	Leave a light and dark grey trail behind the helicopter after 3 seconds.	Stop the game if the helicopter touches a parrot.	Move the helicopter to a start location. Then make it move by following the mouse.	Make the parrot flap its wings by changing costumes.	Change the costumes of the helicopter to make it look like it is flying.

Supporting PREDICT

indefinite loop

Notes on the activity

This optional activity helps pupils to think about the bigger purpose of the program before they start looking at parts of it in later sections.

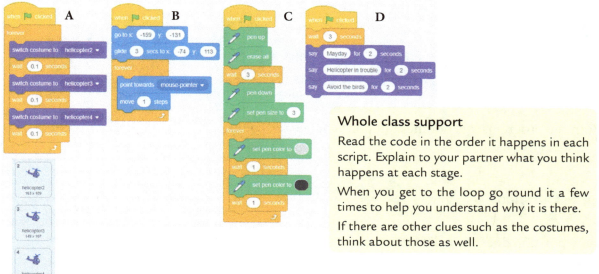

Whole class support

Read the code in the order it happens in each script. Explain to your partner what you think happens at each stage.

When you get to the loop go round it a few times to help you understand why it is there.

If there are other clues such as the costumes, think about those as well.

The reading code questions encourage pupils to read the code carefully so that they will make better predictions below.

Sometimes pupils include the example forever loop in the top right side of the page which technically in not helicopter code but they have correctly identified it so let them have the point if they question it

Reading code

1. How many forever (indefinite) loops are in all of the helicopter code above? 3 (1 mark)

2. What code blocks are **inside** the forever (indefinite) loop in code block B? Point towards mouse pointer & move 1 steps (1 mark)

3. How **many seconds** will code block D run for once the green flag is clicked? 9 seconds (1 mark)

4. How long does it stay **light grey** for before changing to dark grey in code block C? 1 second (1 mark)

Q All Key words have been highlighted in this questions. Encourage pupils to look for key words or similar words in the code.

Q4 Ask if pupils can see light grey or dark grey colours in the code blocks?

Match the code block to the correct prediction. The first one has been done for you.

Read the main program code sections A to D slowly from top to bottom. Beware, there are two false predictions which don't match any code above!

D	C (1 mark)		B (1 mark)		A (1 mark)
Say what has happened to the helicopter and what the user should do in the game.	Leave a light and dark grey trail behind the helicopter after 3 seconds.	Stop the game if the helicopter touches a parrot.	Move the helicopter to a start location. Then make it move by following the mouse.	Make the parrot flap its wings by changing costumes.	Change the costumes of the helicopter to make it look like it is flying.

Helicopter Game
INVESTIGATE
Start Scratch and load
Helicopter

Work with a partner

indefinite loop

Run the code
Play the helicopter game a few times.

Investigate (Run the programs lots of times but don't change the code)

Look at the code inside the helicopter
Helicopter Sprite Questions

1. What x and y position does the helicopter start at?

2. What x and y position does the helicopter glide to 3 seconds after the game has started?

3. How long does it take before the light and dark grey trail starts to show in the game?

Look at the code inside parrot 1
Parrot 1 Sprite Questions

1. How long is parrot 1 hidden for once the game starts?

2. Which two backdrops are only run once the parrot touches a helicopter?

3. How long is there between each beat of the parrot's wings?

4. What does the parrot do once it touches the edge of the screen? What code block instructs it to do that?

Now mark your work using the answer marksheet

photocopiable page

Supporting
INVESTIGATE

Whole class advice

Work in pairs, one device between the pair. Take it in turns every question to swap who runs code. You must work at the same pace as your partner and not move on to the next question until you have both written your answer down. If you disagree, write a different answer. You must mark your work before moving on to the next section.

Notes on the activity

Investigating the code encourages pupils to think deeply about how it works. Check that every pupil is filling in and marking the questions individually but at the pace of the slowest in the pair. Sometimes a pair decides not to mark to speed up their efforts. Marking gives valuable information, so I recommend sending them back to mark their work. A class instruction to come and talk to you if they have over half of the questions wrong or they do not understand the answer after they have marked it helps to check progress is being made correctly. There is real value in collecting these scores to build up a summative picture of pupil progress.

Run the code

Play the helicopter game a few times.

Investigate (Run the programs lots of times but don't change the code)

Look at the code inside the helicopter
Helicopter sprite questions

1. What x and y position does the helicopter start at?
    X: -159 Y: -131 (1 mark)

2. What x and y position does the helicopter **glide** to 3 seconds after the game has started? X -74 Y: 113 (1 mark)

3. How long does it take before the light and dark grey trail starts to show in the game? 3 seconds (1 mark)

Look at the code inside Parrot 1
Parrot 1 Sprite Questions

1. How long is parrot 1 hidden for once the game starts? 5 seconds (1 mark)

2. Which two backdrops are only run once the parrot touches a helicopter?

    Boom & xy-grid (1 mark)

3. How long is there between each beat of the parrot's wings?
    0.5 seconds (1 mark)

4. What does the parrot do once it touches the edge of the screen? What code block instructs it to do that? bounce (1 mark)

Now mark your work using the answer marksheet

Q ALL Are pupils looking at code in the right place? This is a very common error.

Q1 This is initialization code, as it makes the helicopter always start in the same place every time the game is started

Q2 Keyword is glide – can pupils find that in the code?

Q3 Ask pupils which blocks start drawing (pen down) and which blocks stop drawing (pen up) ? How long is the pen up for before it is pen down?

Q1 Ask pupils which blocks hide the parrot and which blocks show the parrot?

Q2 Keyword is backdrop – can pupils find that in the code?

Q3 Costumes.

Q4 Keyword is edge – can pupils find that in the code?

Whole class support

Remind pupils to mark the investigate questions and to report any answers that they still do not understand. It is far easier for a teacher to help at this point than after the lesson.

Helicopter Game CHANGE

Start Scratch and load the Helicopter Game

Work with a partner

indefinite loop

Make small changes to the code

Helicopter Sprite Questions

1. Can you make the smoke trail start earlier? What did you change?

2. Can you make the helicopter move faster? What did you change?

3. Can you make the smoke trail change colour slower? What did you change?

4. Can you make the smoke trail wider? *HINT Pen commands.* What did you change?

5. Can you make the rotor on the helicopter look like it is running slower?
    HINT Run one code section at a time to see which one controls the rotors. What did you change?

Parrot 1 Sprite Questions

1. Can you make the parrot move slower? What did you change?

2. Can you make the wings flap slower? What did you change?

Now mark this page using the marksheet

Supporting
CHANGE

Notes on the activity

Changing or modifying code is a core part of this module, so I suggest you do not leave it out. It is an important step towards creation of their own code as parts they have modified they will feel more ownership of. Recording marks will help with assessment.

Make small changes to the code

Helicopter sprite questions

1. Can you make the smoke trail start earlier? What did you change?

   Either change wait 3 seconds to a lower number or remove the wait 3 seconds block (1 mark)

2. Can you make the helicopter move faster? What did you change?

   Change move 1 step to a higher number (1 mark)

3. Can you make the smoke trail change colour slower? What did you change?

   Change wait 1 seconds to a higher number (1 mark)

4. Can you make the smoke trail wider? *HINT Pen commands* What did you change?

   Change set pen size to a higher number than 3 (1 mark)

5. Can you make the rotor on the helicopter look like it is running slower?
   HINT Run one code section at a time to see which one controls the rotors What did you change?

   Change wait 0.1 seconds to a higher number (1 mark)

Parrot 1 Sprite Questions

1. Can you make the parrot move slower? What did you change?

   Change move 0.7 steps to a lower number such as 0.1 seconds (1 mark)

2. Can you make the wings flap slower? What did you change?

   Change wait 0.5 seconds to a higher number (1 mark)

Q1 What starts the pen drawing? What stops the pen drawing? How long between both?

Q1 Questions about the order of commands test pupils' understanding of sequences.

Q2 Pretend you are in a forever loop moving one step. Now pretend to be moving two steps in the same amount of time.

Q3 Get two felt tips and a sheet of paper. Hold one down and draw for one second. Then hold the other pen down and draw for a further second. Repeat this to show a dashed line. Ask pupils what you would need to do to make the dashes longer without speeding up the drawing.

Q4 Wider is another name for the size of something.

Q5 The rotor is a costume. Look in the costumes tab to help you see what the costumes look like.

Q1 Revising a basic knowledge of tenths helps. 0.7 is splitting 1 second into ten equal parts and then only using seven of them. 0.1 is splitting 1 second into ten equal parts and then only using one of them.

Q1 Even if pupils have never encountered simple decimal fractions like 0.5, changing them in Scratch will help to build up a picture of how these work in a concrete environment.

Q2 Wing flapping is created using costumes.

Whole class support

Apart from the last question, you will only need to change a number to answer each questions. If you change it and it does not do what you want, remember to change it back before examining another option.

Whole class support

Remind pupils to mark the changing code questions and to report any answers that they still do not understand. It is far easier for a teacher to help at this point than after the lesson.

Now mark this page using the marksheet

Helicopter Game
CREATE

Work on
your own

indefinite loop

Design and code your own simple game that uses loops. You can adapt any ideas from the helicopter game.

Idea level *My game will...*

Design level (Draw your game simply. What characters will you use?, What will they do?)

Don't forget initialization How will you return the sprite back to where it was and how it was at the beginning of the game?

Write loop algorithms that you might need (you can write one then code it)

Teacher & Pupil Assessment Circle the stage that you think you have reached in each row. Your teacher will check it.

	Not used a forever loop	Copied a forever loop idea from the helicopter game	Copied and changed a forever loop idea from the helicopter game	Used a forever loop in a way not shown
Indefinite (forever) loops	0 marks	1 mark	2 marks	3 marks
			Not used previous programming concepts for real purpose	Used previous programming concepts for real purpose
Used previous programming concept such as count-controlled loops			0 marks	1 mark
			No theme in planning or code	Has a theme in planning or code
Has a project theme in planning or code			0 marks	1 mark

You can check your progress using the planning and making code marksheet

photocopiable page

E

Supporting
CREATE

Design and code your own simple game that uses loops. You can adapt any ideas from the helicopter game.

Notes on the activity

The make part of a project is really important, and teachers should always make sure that pupils have time to make their own project, even if that means reducing the time spent on other stages for pupils who work slowly. It helps if pupils work on their own for this whilst supporting their partner.

Idea level *My game will...*

Things to check

Has your game got a clear aim? Will someone else understand your aim if they read it here?

Has your aim been clearly shown in the game?

Design level (Draw your game simply. What characters will you use?, What will they do?)

Have you sketched your characters simply?

Have you shown where your characters will start from?

Have you written **simple** notes to explain how things work?

Marking planning is a great way of valuing planning. You may not want to mark planning every time, but it is useful to do on occasions.

If a pupil is really struggling with an aspect of planning, consider modelling a plan based on the helicopter game.

Don't forget initialization How will you return the sprite back to where it was and how it was at the beginning of the game?

Write loop algorithms that you might need (you can write one then code it)

Have you written loop algorithms to show how something works before coding it.

E.g.

Loop always

    Change costume

    Wait a second

Whole class advice

Work on your own, one device each. You can discuss the work with your former partner but you are responsible for creating your own projects. Save your work regularly. Read the instructions carefully. Assess your own work by circling where you think you are in the assessment grid at the bottom of the page.

Warn pupils that you are going to start assessing their work. It is easier to assess during the lesson, when you can ask questions about their work and pupils can answer these. Start assessing roughly 45 minutes before the end of the module. Start with pupils who started their final phase earlier to give late finishers the most amount of time.

Whole class advice

Towards the end of the module, ask pupils to self-assess their work using the three rows at the bottom. Use of indefinite (forever) loops, project theme and use of previous concepts.

Teacher & Pupil Assessment

Circle the stage that you think you have reached in each row. Your teacher will check it.

Have you changed a forever loop idea or made a new one?	Not used a forever loop	Copied a forever loop idea from the helicopter game	Copied and changed a forever loop idea from the helicopter game	Used a forever loop in a way not shown
Indefinite (forever) loops	0 marks	1 mark	2 marks	3 marks

Have you added a count-controlled loop for a real reason to gain an extra mark?		Not used previous programming concepts for real purpose	Used previous programming concepts for real purpose
Used previous programming concept such as count-controlled loops		0 marks	1 mark

Has your game got a clear theme or purpose?		No theme in planning or code	Has a theme in planning or code
Has a project theme in planning or code		0 marks	1 mark

You can check your progress using the planning and making code marksheet

FLOW Marksheet

1. Find the forever loop and tick all the blocks inside the loop.
2. Draw a line to show the order the code will be run in. Draw dots to show actions. One has been done for you.

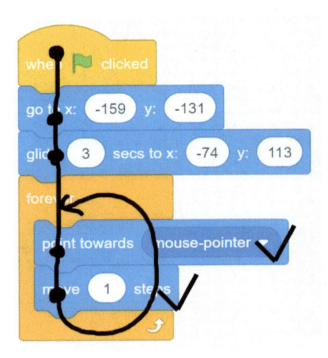

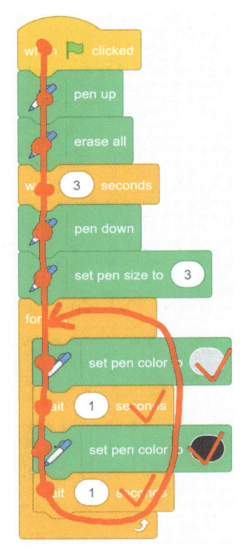

(1 mark) for the loop drawn as shown
(1 mark) for the dots drawn as shown
(1 mark) for all the ticks

(1 mark) for the loop drawn as shown
(1 mark) for the dots drawn as shown
(1 mark) for all the ticks

photocopiable page

Helicopter Game
PREDICT
Marksheet

Reading code

1. How many forever (indefinite) loops are in all of the helicopter code above?
   3 (1 mark)

2. What code blocks are inside the forever (indefinite) loop in code block B?
   Point towards mouse pointer & move 1 steps (1 mark)

3. How many seconds will code block D run for once the green flag is clicked?
   9 seconds (1 mark)

4. How long does it stay light grey for before changing to dark grey in code block C?
   1 second (1 mark)

Match the code block to the correct prediction. The first one has been done for you.

Read the main program code sections A to D slowly from top to bottom. Beware, there are two false predictions which don't match any code above!

D	C (1 mark)		B (1 mark)		A
Say what has happened to the helicopter and what the user should do in the game.	Leave a light and dark grey trail behind the helicopter after 3 seconds.	Stop the game if the helicopter touches a parrot.	Move the helicopter to a start location. Then make it move by following the mouse.	Make the parrot flap its wings by changing costumes.	Change the costumes of the helicopter to make it look like it is flying. (1 mark)

119

Helicopter Game
INVESTIGATE
Marksheet

Look at the code inside the helicopter
Helicopter Sprite Questions

1. What x and y position does the helicopter start at?
    X: -159 Y: -131 (1 mark)

2. What x and y position does the helicopter glide to 3 seconds after the game has started?
    X -74 Y: 113 (1 mark)

3. How long does it take before the light and dark grey trail starts to show in the game?
    3 seconds (1 mark)

Look at the code inside parrot 1
Parrot 1 Sprite Questions

1. How long is parrot 1 hidden for once the game starts?
    5 seconds (1 mark)

2. Which two backdrops are only run once the parrot touches a helicopter?
    Boom & xy-grid (1 mark)

3. How long is there between each beat of the parrot's wings?
    0.5 seconds (1 mark)

4. What does the parrot do once it touches the edge of the screen? What code block instructs it to do that?
    bounce (1 mark)

**Helicopter Game
CHANGE
Marksheet**

**Make small changes to the code
Helicopter Sprite Questions**

1. Can you make the smoke trail start earlier?
What did you change?

Either change wait 3 seconds to a lower number or remove the wait 3 seconds block (1 mark)

2. Can you make the helicopter move faster?
What did you change?

Change move 1 step to a higher number (1 mark)

3. Can you make the smoke trail change colour slower?
What did you change?

Change wait 1 seconds to a higher number (1 mark)

4. Can you make the smoke trail wider?
HINT Pen commands. What did you change?

Change set pen size to a higher number than 3 (1 mark)

5. Can you make the rotor on the helicopter look like it is running slower?
HINT Run one code section at a time to see which one controls the rotors What did you change?

Change wait 0.1 seconds to a higher number (1 mark)

Parrot 1 Sprite Questions
1. Can you make the parrot move slower?
What did you change?

Change move 0.7 steps to a lower number such as 0.1 seconds (1 mark)

2. Can you make the wings flap slower?
What did you change?

Change wait 0.5 seconds to a higher number (1 mark)

Now mark this page using the marksheet

photocopiable page

Helicopter game
CREATE
Prompt sheet

Design and code your own simple game that uses loops. You can adapt any ideas from the helicopter game.

Idea level *My game will…*

Things to check

Has your game got a clear aim? Will someone else understand your aim if they read it here?

Has your aim been clearly shown in the game?

Design Level (Draw your game simply. What characters will you use? What will they do?)

Have you sketched your characters simply?

Have you shown where your characters will start from?

Have you written **simple** notes to explain how things work?

Don't forget initialization How will you return the sprite back to where it was and how it was at the beginning of the game?

Write loop algorithms that you might need (you can write one then code it)

Have you written loop algorithms to show how something works before coding it. E.g. Loop always Change costume Wait a second			

Teacher & Pupil Assessment Circle the stage that you think you have reached in each row. Your teacher will check it.

Have you changed a forever loop idea or made a new one?	Not used a forever loop	Copied a forever loop idea from the helicopter game	Copied and changed a forever loop idea from the helicopter game	Used a forever loop in a way not shown
Indefinite (forever) loops	0 marks	1 mark	2 marks	3 marks

Have you added a count-controlled loop for a real reason to gain an extra mark?	Not used previous programming concepts for real purpose	Used previous programming concepts for real purpose
Used previous programming concept such as count-controlled loops	0 marks	1 mark

Has your game got a clear theme or purpose?	No theme in planning or code	Has a theme in planning or code
Has a project theme in planning or code	0 marks	1 mark

E

www.ingramcontent.com/pod-product-compliance
Lightning Source LLC
LaVergne TN
LVHW082347060326

832902LV00017B/2708